"My friend, Kevin Murray, is an unusually creative thinker who has wrestled for years with great writers and profound ideas. His *Encourage to Faith* portrays an engaging, whimsical, and compelling spiritual journey that led him to Jesus and continues to draw him to the Father's house. As Kevin puts it, it is his "restless desire to find God in eternity through the constraints of the temporal." Through a series of insightful observations on life, growing up, the quest for identity, and the role of pain, he builds a cogent case that "the scoffers don't get the last word, the lovers do."
-Dr. Ken Boa
Author, President, Reflections Ministries

"Armed with an inquisitive mind and analytical disposition, Kevin Murray describes his spiritual quest for the elixir of life. His odyssey takes him through a cafeteria of humanistic "isms" which by God's grace ends when at age 36 he encounters Christ as the lodestar to the true meaning and purpose of his life. I found this compendium of his musings studded with practical insights and timely encouragements for fellow travelers seeking an abiding faith in Christ."
-George Yacoubian, PH.D.
Retired senior teacher of Biblical Studies at The Westminster Schools, Atlanta, GA.

"Kevin Murray's wit and charm come through in this deeply satisfying encouragement wrapped in a memoir."
-Scott Frey
Founder and CEO, PossibleNow

Encourage To Faith

Encourage To Faith

The Presumptuous, Mostly Accurate Account of
One Man's Journey into the Heart of God

KEVIN MURRAY

ISBN-13: 9780692808849
ISBN-10: 0692808841
Library of Congress Control Number: 2016919171
Kindred Travelers Press, Safety Harbor, FL

Special thanks to Jessie Marshall for her invaluable copyediting services, not to mention her God-given patience.

Kindred Travelers Press™

To Dad,
and to Uncle Jack,
who now knows more than those of us still waiting

Contents

Preface

This is not a book about theological answers or specialized jargon from seminary books. It is not based on so-called conventional thinking. It is my own thinking, and it is a simple book about faith.

There is no way I can fulfill the title, "Encourage To Faith." I like to exhort, but I can't deliver anyone *to* faith. That's God's role. I'm just another person in the stands rooting for the team. It is God above Who not only cheers us on, but also accomplishes the goal of drawing us to Himself.[1] My joyful role is but to come alongside and share what I've learned on my journey into His heart. That's what this book is about.

I feel much more qualified to fulfill the promise in the subtitle: that of being presumptuous—no revelation there. The telling of my story is undoubtedly as presumptuous as it gets. I'm presuming there is a chance you may find my journey of interest, at least those parts which overlap with your own. But I apologize in advance if at any time I seem to be saying my journey is yours. There are as many different journeys as there are people who come to Christ.

Ours can be parallel but never the same. God sets the way, but we, as kindred travelers, must each make our own pilgrimages.

As God would have it, our journeys have intersected here. I don't take that lightly. In the pages that follow, I promise to do my best to keep the tale fresh and rolling along, and, most importantly, not to trifle with such matters as are near and dear to every heart. We all have a story to tell. I assure you there will be tears in the telling of mine.

And in the process of sharing the deepest ravines of my heart, I fully expect to give a mostly accurate account. Allow me to explain:

Throughout the writing I reserve the right to use Bible verses—which I take to be the inspired, inerrant, and holy Word of God—as much or as little as springs to mind. Also, I may or may not use copious amounts of quotes from authors of renown and repute, or ill repute, depending on my mood. These too will be 100 percent accurate, if not in their original sense, in the recitation and credit I give to them. They also make me sound brainier than I am, which I like. I read often, widely, and hopefully, deeply enough that I learn from those who preceded me. But how that fits into the retelling of a story like this, God only knows, and I will only find out as I move through the rewinding of the emotional archives.

I also reserve the right to make liberal use of bad puns, snide remarks, and jumbled colloquialisms where accuracy is neither here nor there. When I'm done I hope it will make at least a lick of sense.

Further, some of the time I will be speaking in the voices of metaphor and simile as is my wont. I am drawn to these like a bee before a profusion of flowers—see what I mean? And in their application I invoke the privilege that they *not* make perfect sense, if that helps them to make heart-sense.

In all, spontaneity requires that I not put conventional constraints on the writing. You want authenticity? My heart? The truth? Then it has to lean toward my preferred stream of consciousness mode or I will fall the other way into the creativity-stifling abyss—unpleasant business, that. It is for this same reason I chose the topics and their order as I have, both of which may seem random to the reader, but are not to me. And if I say that often and with enough confidence you too might start to believe it.

At best this whole writing process is an imperfect art, simply the best way I know to relay what I feel on the inside and get it to the outside in a form as untainted as the barriers of the mind will allow. And all this for the benefit of any who may find it mildly interesting, useful, or even pathetic and reassuring in a boy-at-least-I'm-not-as-messed-up-as-him kind of way.

I won't even attempt to present a tidy, orderly, or systematic detail of how God moved first to my mind and then into my heart over these many years. This for the simple reason that how the heart receives love is not any of those things, nor is it supposed to be. If you agree with that, perhaps you'll accept that there is a method to my madness, which in this case will be to tell it as it comes, not as the successive steps of faith-born epiphanies, but rather as a collage of them all. When the tide rolls in we don't see which is the first grain of sand to get wet, we just know the whole of the beach gets a bath. I believe that's how God works in all of us. At least that's how it happened to me.

Surely by now you realize I lean more lyricist than grammarian, and so I reserve the right to be mostly accurate with my syntax—to play fast and loose with the orthodox rules as is my bent in all walks of life. We all have our biases. George Beverly Shey, the great baritone for evangelist Billy Graham for so many years, told the story about the time he was in London singing, "It took a miracle to put the stars in place."[2] Not long after, a woman wrote a letter to the ministry saying, "I loved your soloist's singing, but it's a bit presumptuous to say that America put the stars in place." "I've tried to watch my diction ever since," Shey said.

Well, in the writing of this book I'll try to watch mine, as well as my biases, which owe their particular existence to my being born in the United States of America at a relatively safe and snug yet morally shifting time in history, in the era of the baby boomers, as the baby of the family, and brought up in the casual climes of the warm southeast in a good, middle-class family. Many of these details will likely differ from yours and that's okay. I believe at the core we are all made of the same stuff. We have the same origin and the same innate desire to discover our destiny, to seek the answers to this life.

I realize the answers and conclusions that I've reached may not be accurate to everyone's way of thinking. I can only hope that what I have to say will resonate still. Because I assure you, relative to my heart it is all accurate. This is my journey into the heart of God.

Kevin Murray, 2016

INTRODUCTION

I didn't know that I was on any sort of journey at first, not for the first thirty-six years of my life I didn't. A thinkful amble, certainly, but not a journey. Curiously though, I did feel lost, which told me there was a journey to be had. During no part of all those years did life make sense, not deep down. It was that way from the get-go, full as it all began with family and warm beds, good relationships near and far, small yards and big parks, friends and dogs, dragonflies, bougainvilleas, bikes and bullies, skinned knees, and banged up lunch boxes always filled with care. And I did all my ambling about under the slow cotton clouds of south, south Florida.

A good start to a tangible life. But what did it matter?

Grade school comforts became junior high stresses, followed by an escape to the red clay of Georgia at an age when esteem is most in doubt. New cultures and causes ensued—girls, that is— high school, college, mostly pointless. I hung on, happy but disengaged, sad but at least directed some which way. Then more girls, The Girl, marriage, kids, life—for which I believed there could be an answer, but for the life of me I didn't know what it was. And that mindset is called coping, which beats merely surviving. And thanks be to God for the blessings just the same. But I didn't know Him then. So as I say, what did it matter?

My recollection of dwelling on that deepest of thoughts that we all have goes back as early as age five, and it seems for thirty-one more years I couldn't accept the possibility that there was no answer. It all had to all make sense. I couldn't move forward until it did. So there I dwelled. And while I didn't have any peace that I was getting anywhere, at least I knew I wasn't going in circles, more like inescapable meanderings, the kind where I was always accumulating more and more information, gobbling up and covering new ground. The philosopher in me rather loved that. Pondering anything and everything is what philosophers do. Yes, let's gather all the pieces of the existence puzzle to see where we fit in shall we?

And as I stacked together pyramids of promising ideas, I cast aside the useless globs and banished from my consideration all that was plainly unable to fill my deepest need before returning to and holding up for closer inspection those which held the most promise, sort of like pushing aside the garnish to get to the filet mignon.

My litmus test was always, "Is it true? Is it logical? Will it bring me closer to resolving The Big Q, which for me, and for all of us, is, 'What is the meaning of life?'" Or more egocentrically stated: "Why am I here?"

As I grew into the older version of my younger philosopher-self, I increasingly processed outwardly what I had previously deliberated only on the inside. And so those lucky souls closest to me got to hear countless variations of my latest philosophical discoveries. The older I got I became more assured and emphatic about my opinions, but the truth was that those opinions I proclaimed most definitively—the kind you end with, "Period, end of sentence"—were actually the ones most deserving of triple question marks. Yes, it must be said that after more than three decades of life I had so far resolved only this: All we can know for sure is that we're born, we live, we die. Period. Exclamation point.

Kind of dispiriting, wouldn't you say? But in the interest of proving I am an exhorter at heart, I will jump ahead and tell you:

This is a book about a quest.

This is a book about a surrender.

This is a book about coming to terms with who I am.

This is a book about encouragement.

This is a book about a journey into the heart of God.

This is an incomplete book about what I have learned so far.

Or have I learned it?

The more I write, I'm not sure if I have really learned all I claim. How much of it has stuck after all? I make the same mistakes now that I made when I was five. I ate too much ice cream then, I eat too much now. I was impatient when I couldn't get my toy race cars to work then, and I'm impatient when stuck in traffic now. I liked dogs then, I like them now—that's not relevant, I just wanted you to know I like dogs. I wanted every toy in the five-and-dime store then and pouted when my mother wouldn't comply (thanks Mom), and I buy more stuff than I need now. I believed in ghosts then, and I believe in them now, though a different kind (but I'm getting ahead of myself). I'm also just getting started. I got mad when I lost at board games then, still do now. I had a low tolerance for pain that bordered on the hypochondriacal then, still do now, though my cold is almost gone. I argued routinely with my older brother then, who was always wrong by the way, and I argue with those who disagree with my politics and positions now. I didn't wear seat belts then—didn't have to—and I don't wear them now. Okay that's not true *or* relevant, other than to say, things have changed. Back then times were simpler, but the essence was the same. We ate, we slept, we related, we learned. Life is basic at its core. And governments are wonderful and always make life better. That's not true either, but I didn't know that when I was five.

All in all I had my foibles then and, in short, I'm still a bit of a crumb, Jesus help me. And there you have it. Those words just poured out of me, a revelation from me to myself. I think they might even be the hidden title of this book: "Jesus Help Me." It is my subconscious recognition that He alone can. Because life without God is a struggle, and the only way out of the quandary is to journey into His heart. A journey not of dry morsels for the intellect, but refreshment for the soul. One of grace and rescue, advancement by fits and starts, through hope and dismay, in times of pain and joy. It is not for the foolhardy, but it is for the desperate. This I knew when I accepted Christ, when, even though I lacked more answers than I held, still I plunged.

That's what we're going to do.

Part One

SEEKING THE HEART

Chapter 1

GIVE IT TO ME STRAIGHT

*The heart has its reasons of which
reason knows nothing.*

BLAISE PASCAL

Why am I here? Not everybody can answer that for themselves. But I can. "Impossible to answer!" some will protest. "At least in any real sense." "You just suck it up and put one foot in front of the other in this life, fella." Those who say so would likely suppose the motivation behind my claim to be hubris with a splash of weakness. But I say it's faith with a full-blown soak in the Water of Life.

Yes, in my enthusiasm I've broken protocol. We've hardly begun and already I'm jumping ahead to the evangelical pinnacle of our story. Already the Water of Life and I haven't even set the table with talk of struggle and triumph, a wayward will and a fall, and triumph again. You're supposed to save the best for last, I've been told. Where are the penetrating anecdotes? The woebegone tales and stories grand that properly sweep us step by arduous step up the mountain of faith? Patience. They're either coming or there aren't any—you'll be the judge. Either way, I assure you that this is only an ordinary story. One of finding love and purpose in the heart of a God Who so happens to bring about the miracles I needed all along. In other words, it is the best kind of story.

Why am I here? I could have answered, "I don't know." Perhaps a satisfactory answer to the naysayers, but it would not be true, not anymore. I do have an answer, it's just that not everybody wants to hear it.

Why am I here? God in His kindness chose to make me so that I could enter into the heart of Jesus. Too general? A bit of of a bailout? Not so. Not when one understands that to question "Why am I here?" implies there is an answer. It is a crying out to the light from the dark, a reaching out from an answerless world to the God Who made everything. It is not as the world would tell us, a bunch of woofing at nothing. That's what the answerless always want us to believe. They want us to join them in their defeat. But I chose the route of the optimist, to act. And that was the pinnacle moment of my life: reaching out of the darkness and believing a hand would reach for mine. I was not disappointed.

Why am I here? Because God made the world to spin, set the tides, and gave atoms their electrical charge, and then made me to be His adopted son.

Why am I here? Because of a gift—the privilege of being a part of what my Savior is doing through His body here on earth until He comes again and takes me to be with Him for all eternity.

That's why.

Chapter 2

THE EARLY SOJOURNER

The simplest solution is often the best.

OCCAM'S RAZOR

I was six, maybe seven, and for days I'd been looking forward to going with my new friend and next door neighbor Karen Siever to appear on the local live TV program, *The Banjo Billy Show*, and now I was there. It was a popular kids' show that aired after *Captain Kangaroo* as I recall, and it was a Miami institution, somewhat along the lines of the *Howdy Doody* historical marker.

As we sat in the studio bleachers, we reached the part of the show where Banjo Billy passes his black derby hat around to each of the twenty or so children in the audience to see who picks out the winning number and wins the day's big prize. I was first. I looked in and saw maybe two dozen folded pieces of paper, each the size of my finger tip, one of which had a conspicuous piece of gold tape holding it shut. So I did what I do—I reasoned, "That one won't be the winning one. Too obvious. Not elegant enough." Though those words were no doubt simplified in my mind to, "They're tryin' to trick us."

I picked one without the tape and the hat moved down the line. Karen Siever was sitting next to me and I watched her as, without hesitation, she reached for the one with the gold tape. Her prize for choosing the winning number was a giant Black Cow Sucker, a coveted hard caramel candy that she ate by herself the whole long ride home, while I drooled.

That one event typifies much of my childhood—my entire life actually—except for the drooling part. I was always looking for the elegant solution. Without it life didn't feel right. It's not as hopelessly idealistic as it may seem. It has its practical points. First, as I was to find out much later, the elegant solution does exist. And second, the worn path of the lemmings has been known to lead off a high cliff. But it also has one very costly bad point: I have routinely missed the simple and obvious for much of my life. When the lemmings head for the nearest exit during a fire, it might be a good idea to follow. Sometimes the elegant solution and the simple one are one and the same.

I was an inquiring sort, wired with a drive to know truth and meaning. Give me the truth; tell my why I'm here. They are two sides of the same coin and proof that I was a philosopher at heart, and a strange kid. I liked knowledge, but not as much as I liked thinking about knowledge— to see what was behind the curtain, so to speak. Yes, all paths led there for me. I confess I thought every day about those things, in between climbing trees or playing army man in the front yard or eating bowlfuls of sugary cereal or watching cartoons or playing dodge ball or turning in English homework or not turning in math homework. In other words, normally I was normal.

But there's no getting away from the fact that I liked to ponder anything and everything. Would I prefer to die on the open plains of Africa by a vicious lion attack or in the back corner of the closet by a thousand scorpion stings? You know, fun stuff like that. At other times, when I wasn't conjuring scenarios of morbidity, I pondered simple things like—well, like infinity.

I recall the circumstances when I first heard about the concept—who knows from where, probably on the school playground. I burst through the front door already halfway through asking my mother to explain it. She tried, but being of a more practical nature, I don't think it was nearly as big a deal to her. So she gave me the bare-bones version, "Infinity is something that never ends," then turned back to her cooking. Never ends, huh?

That night I looked out my bedroom window at all the stars and picked one as far to the east as I could see, then drew an imaginary line to the farthest one I could find in the west, then I imagined the line continuing both ways without ever stopping. Infinity. "That must be how God is," I thought. It is my first recollection of contemplating God, and the thought hung there for nearly three decades.

The following day I set that thought aside and resumed my daily routine of punctuating every hour spent in age-appropriate kid stuff with at least a dozen abstract thoughts: Who invented math? How do people stand upside down in China? Why doesn't the world fall?—turns out it did—Why didn't Karen Siever share her candy with me?

So much talk about thoughts, you might wonder about my feelings; namely if I had them. Yes, very much so, oftentimes happy ones. But my conclusions about the world around me, or lack thereof, also brought about other feelings. I wasn't a morose stick in the mud, but when not absorbed in deep thoughts, my feelings did trend toward the fearful, restless, or sad variety. In all, my feelings were not safe to me, I believe, because I felt unsafe. I don't mean at home; it wasn't that. It was much worse. I felt unsafe in the world.

And once I saw that my feelings worked against me, I used my thoughts to push the whole bundle of them down until I could sort it all out. Wouldn't you know I'm still working on those confounded feelings today. Looking back now, it's easy to see they're what drove me onward, though I suppose I wasn't prewired to access my feelings without running them past my mind first. Nevertheless, I did my best to adapt and learned to plumb their shallows, leaving the deeper matters for my thoughts.

Times were safer back then and I roamed a lot by myself, often walking the labyrinthine sidewalks connecting the neighborhoods of Miami and counting steps to rest my mind. I had a hundred such diversions for that same reason. At least I wasn't obsessive about it—it took 512 steps to circle my block in case you were wondering. Unfortunately, after many years and hundreds of laps around the block, I still had no answer for the meaning of life. In short, other than brief interludes of food, sleep, and play, my childhood can be summarized thus: I observed and thought, played and thought, then contemplated why I thought what I thought. In fact I haven't stopped. That was my realm of comfort then and it still is today.

I've always tried to step back to observe the whole of life, including myself, in an effort toward objectivity. As a kid, I lived and breathed as if there was such a thing as ultimate truth. I needed it to be so. I understood that if there wasn't...well, I'm at a loss for words to describe the feeling it gave me, though "surreal" comes close. Or how about this? If there wasn't an ultimate truth, I was a leaf blowing through the woods without a tree. Yes, I think that describes it. At least I was feeling the wind, even if I didn't know where I came from or was going.

You come to awareness in this world that you're in a family, in a home, not knowing how you got there, just that you recognize these faces around you. Then you grow up, learn rules and customs, branch out to the wider world, learn some more, and somehow that's supposed to make you feel you have a place in the world. Oh yeah, and after an indeterminate time you die. Encouraged yet? I wasn't either.

I couldn't get any of it out of my head. But that didn't keep me from enjoying a good childhood, complete with a block full of friends and a brother to join me in my mischief, an outgoing father who knew how to provide and tell a good joke—though he did have a meticulously disciplinarian streak and would charge me a dime every time I left a light on—and a mother, liked by all, who took care of "her boys" and made the best homemade cookies in town. And whenever I got myself too worked up over my habitual forlornness, I took refuge in a sea of books. I learned early on that my thoughts and feelings pulled together and not apart whenever I read the Dr. Seuss series or *Mother Goose's Nursery Rhymes*. The big world might have been confusing, but these made sense. Better still, these made time stop.

Chapter 3

AGAINST THE WIND

Tomorrow, and tomorrow, and tomorrow,
Creeps in this petty pace from day to day,
To the last syllable of recorded time;
And all our yesterdays have lighted fools
The way to dusty death. Out, out, brief candle!

WILLIAM SHAKESPEARE,
MACBETH

When we've been there ten thousand
years, bright shining as the sun,
We've no less days to sing God's praise
than when we've first begun.

JOHN NEWTON, "AMAZING GRACE"

L ife is short. Life is forever. It is both, don't you think? Don't worry, I'm not going to wax Einsteinian here and start in on the Theory of Relativity. Forever wasn't a part of that anyway.

When I was ten, sometimes life felt like it would last forever. Long Florida summers lazed in from the east and settled merrily onshore. Then school got here and summer had hardly happened, *fssst-wisssh*, gone. It just slid back into the Atlantic like one of my poorly-constructed sand castles, and my carefree days along with it.

On second thought, I don't know how carefree they really were, since true to form, I spent inordinate time thinking of time. Not the ticking clock variety. I was more interested in the long view—lifetimes, millennia, eternity. My go-to mental image was that of a calendar with the twelve months joined in a circle. In my mind, to go forward a month was a counterclockwise motion and to go back, clockwise. Not sure why, other than maybe I sensed that to go forward in my own life I needed to go back.

These days I still use that circular calendar image, but there's also a new image—a day-to-day calendar that sits on the sill of an open window where the wind blows past, in increasingly stronger gusts, till the pages fly off one by one and disappear into the sky and it all becomes a blur. That wind is real; it is the specter of eternity and it comes to whisk the time away. Depending on your age you know what I'm taking about.

Growing up, the oldest person I knew was my maternal grandmother, Grandmom to me. Her house was full of Zane Grey novels, old clocks, and dog fur, and I rather enjoyed it there. I'd study her in her rocking chair as she watched her westerns and wonder about all those calendar cycles she had been through. She was born in 1900, sixty years before my arrival, and too many revolutions for my mind to track.

To grab hold, I'd try to widen my own lifeline, stretch it like a rubber band to gain a sense of how it feels to live as long as she. But in the process of widening my view, I'd always lose focus of the narrow everyday parts. Squinting helped. I'd imagine various scenes of her going through all of life's experiences—grade school in a small clapboard building in turn-of-the-century Savannah, traveling about town in a horse-drawn carriage pre-automobile, television still decades away, silent films not here yet, electricity only barely, same with the telephone. After a while I'd switch back to the long view to process it all—my version of trying to feel it—and all those details would suddenly disappear, *snap*, gone.

It was frustrating. I was hoping to find the *why* of life inside this concept of time but could never get my head around it. The whole process was a lot like that optical illusion where you see in the drawing either an old woman's face—eerily similar to the lady in the lunch room at Cypress Elementary, God rest her soul—or the profile of a beautiful young lady, but never both in the same instant. In the end the long view always won out, no doubt bolstered by an inexhaustible need I had to understand my place in history, in this world, in my house, but mostly in my shoes. Besides, the ticking clock reminded me of death.

I recall doing another mind experiment—they never ended with me—right after I turned ten, the big one-oh, where I would imagine going back in time in ten-year increments, now able by measures to gain a perspective on the ten years prior to my birth. And much like a giant measuring rod, I'd tumble decades end-over-end in my mind to reach into the past. I still use that technique by the way. Only as I get older, the measuring rod lengthens and I can see further and further back. Ten, fifty, a hundred, a thousand years. Who knew aging could be so much fun?

As a child I wanted desperately to experience history close-up, for its winds to brush by and seem near. I wanted to transcend time, though I wouldn't have expressed it that way. Regardless, it never happened. I could get close to pretending the sensation but it was never the real thing—*snap*. Like I say, it was frustrating. I didn't know it yet, but when you're born in the natural, into the temporal realm, and onto a terrestrial-sized sundial, what I was attempting was downright impossible. Still I was drawn to it even if I didn't know why. I hadn't learned yet that there was a supernatural way in which it was very possible. All I knew then was that I was born onto the mortal plain, nothing more. One day I wasn't, then in an instant I was. And so from the most personal of vantage points, everything before 1960 was and would remain prehistorical and, hence, inaccessible, and that bedeviled me.

As a Christian, these many tumbling decades later, I am still learning to live with both the wind and the ticking clock, to let them pass by without my clutching or making a possession of either one. I'm doing better. These days when I sense eternity brush past—which is often—I don't try to pin it down; I know I'll never see it that way. Instead I look for its signposts. Love is the biggest. It transcends this world and confirms that the wind is real, and I am drawn perpetually to follow it to its source. The sensation is mysterious yet undeniable for us all, though some resist. It's hard for mortal men to reconcile the temporal with an eternal God. I know I'll never get my arms around it in this world, partly because I'm reluctant to let this world go.

I don't understand how some people prefer the temporal. I know I don't. It's just that old habits die hard.

—◊◊—

Today I'm imagining in a future direction—the upcoming wedding of my daughter. I turn it over in my mind to savor it. I see the walk down the aisle, the happiness spread across her face, her beauty, the celebration around her, and yes, ladies, the gown (men, hang in there; we'll get to you). When the wedding is over the expectation will be realized, no longer only imagined. I've done this before with another daughter and so I know it won't be easy. There will be a profound sense of loss, even as I'm happy for her.

I relate to the movie *Father of the Bride*. After all the planning and festivities, the tension and excitement, and the bill (see men,

I remembered you), the camera slowly pans across the room as the father sits before an empty reception. Alone with his thoughts, he stares into the past and watches his daughter grow up all over again. It all happened so fast.

And now I, like him, see the life of my daughter skip through my imagination and across my heart: holding her when she was seconds old and falling in love right then, running alongside for her first bike ride, the excitement in her eyes on the first day of school, all the birthday parties and good friendships, always her beautiful laugh, then it was off to college and that was that. She was always my child but never a possession. It took a while to learn that. Here for two minutes, soon to be married and gone—into the winds. As I say, it won't be easy.

It can't just be me. Each newborn child is a promising life. The potential for much joy lies ahead and it's all so poignant, yes? But we also know the bumpy road they have to travel. None of us get to stand still in this life. Children grow up, houses are built, houses fall, and people die. That is a mixed blessing if ever there was one. Yet it is not the complete experience. That can only be lived when we are in our true home with God, together with all our loved ones in Christ where "there will no longer be any death; there will no longer be any mourning, or crying, or pain" (Revelation 21:4). Till then, we're left with these short snippets of emotional highs, signposts of eternity that make our happiness both present and full, though we know in the next moment they'll be gone.

Eternity is a gentle wind and I miss it even when it's here.

One recent morning I walked in eternity. I was in the middle of my prayers and it lasted less than a minute. Though I couldn't see God with my eyes, I experienced His immanent presence in a more tangible way than I ever had before. The best way I can put it is that He made Himself visible to my soul. He was as present to me as if He were standing right in front of me, and I felt a comfort and peace I'd never known. I wish I could say this was the norm, or that it lasted longer. Even still in those few moments, God reassured me of all I needed to know, and I understood deep in my soul that everything, from my present troubles to the world's mischief, would be okay.

After it was over, I startled myself by speaking these words out loud: "Everything you've known by faith in Christ is true!" I had experienced the long view, several successive moments as it happens—such a blessed duration, and more than enough. But confound it! By the afternoon where did those feelings go? A mere four hours later and it was a dimming memory, not a present experience. I spent the rest of the day facing the wind like mad, but it was no longer blowing.

The barrier between me and my coveted goal, the full persistent experience of God, is not time itself, but rather my restless desire to find God in eternity through the constraints of the temporal. I live in both realms: His Spirit resides in me now *and* I desire "to be absent from the body and to be at home with the Lord" (2 Corinthians 5:8). That's not a paradox; it's a predicament. And it tells me something promising about my faith.

C.S. Lewis, the ultimate romantic rationalist as he has been called, wrote about that something: "Do fish complain of the sea for being wet? Or if they did, would that fact itself strongly suggest that they had not always been, or would not always be, purely aquatic creatures? Notice how we are perpetually *surprised* by Time. ('How time flies! Fancy John being grown up and married! I can hardly believe it!') In heaven's name, why? Unless, indeed, there is something in us which is *not* temporal."[3]

I sensed this when I was a child, sensed it as an adult before coming to Christ, and I experienced it firsthand during my prayers on that recent morning when I transcended the limitations of a ticking clock and entered the heart of its Maker.

—⁓—

Generational conversation:

Dad: Son, when I was your age I had to push my bicycle uphill in the snow all the way to school.

Son: Gee Pop, seems like it might have been better to leave it at home.

Who do we think we're fooling? I'm not as good as I used to be and even then I wasn't. Same goes for everything else, for the past isn't all it's cracked up to be. People had problems then, we have them now, and we can expect more in the future. Every generation lectures its youth about how they don't appreciate the things of the past, even as the current generation thinks their elders are misguided and stodgy, and so look to the future to solve their problems.

Then they arrive there and they're the ones complaining to any youth who will listen and the cycle repeats. The merry-go-round spins and spins, really fast.

Anyone who has lived twenty years has already learned that each decade gets faster. The first five years of my life might as well have been twenty. By ten, an ant carrying a grasshopper's leg would occupy my mind for a few minutes, or an hour, I couldn't have told you which—time lingered. Ten to twenty was faster, but with all that happened it still seemed a long time. Twenty to thirty—two blips and a wink and it was over, and I had a college degree, a wife, four children, and a mortgage to prove it happened. Thirty to forty—the kids were guided missiles readying for college. You can't be serious! Forty to fifty—blip-*fsst*. Empty nesters who looked at each other and said, what in the world was that? And the wind hits you square in the face. Fifty to sixty—I'll get back to you after my nap. Sixty and beyond—I'll paraphrase a line I heard from comedian Billy Crystal who said, "And by old age you find yourself shuffling around a mall in south Florida, muttering, 'How come the kids don't call, how come the kids don't call?'"

Well, I just finished my nap, and I'm not muttering yet, but I sure do reflect in giddy proportions on the past. When a kid does it it's odd behavior. "Shouldn't Johnny be out climbing trees?" Later in life it's called nostalgia. It is one of life's purely pleasing diversions—romanticizing the past. It's innate in every man for we all descended from the same two who once upon a time had it all—Paradise with God; can't have Paradise without Him. That was before things went terribly wrong. "Paradise Lost," Milton called it, and God's children have longed to get back to that Paradise ever since.

Nostalgia, I believe, is our way of leaning into the rueful acceptance that life has to roll on by. At least it's my way. I do a lot of leaning. I yearn for everything I ever enjoyed or wanted to enjoy but missed. I'm sure that's why I watch grainy old black and white movies, why I read ancient history, and why I went back to visit my childhood home some forty years later.

I made my trip to the past for the same reason I always do: It's wearying in the present, compulsively digging through the fragments of a lifetime to uncover a soul. So off I went to find me even though I knew it wouldn't work. I recognized the place immediately, but it didn't have the foggiest notion who I was, nor did the squatters playing basketball in *my* driveway—the wrong way mind you.

The huge cherry hedges were gone, and the squatters, or current residents if I have to be nice, walked unencumbered into Mr. Mancuso's yard to retrieve their wayward shots. All wrong. Number one, you're supposed to be tearing another hole in your cheap T-shirt while digging the ball out from underneath the dense foliage of poking limbs, then you eat at least one ripe red cherry, ideally two, while you are in there; and two, you never walk on Mr. Mancuso's perfect lawn, ever! Who knows what other breaches in tradition occurred routinely with these guys.

Nevertheless, I admit they seemed amiable enough and I thought it best to be exceedingly friendly in return, realizing it was my only chance at getting an invitation to revisit the inside of my long-ago home and home of my heart still. We exchanged the customary pleasantries and I told them I used to live there as a child. Then I asked if it still had the speckled terrazzo floors inside, and the pale yellow Formica counters with the burn spot, and the cobbled together bookshelves built by my dad and me out of painted two-by-fours and bent over nails, hoping they'd catch the hint. Silent stares told me what I needed to know.

I drove on to my old school and walked the ball fields of my youth, but curiously couldn't find a single plaque commemorating my kickball prowess, the athletic summit from which I leveraged almost half a century of stories grand. Nor could I find the expansive fields that to my memory might as well have been great plains of blowing wheat, where to traverse them was an adventure of Tom Sawyerian proportions (try saying that three times). It had shrunk. Weeds on a sandy lot. And time marches on.

I see I've grown maudlin here. I should know better by now. When I try to tap a glory I pretended to live back then, it's always bittersweet. In the end, returning to the idols of memory is just another way of filling up with the world. I'm not talking about healthy reminiscing over the good parts of growing up that we all have—those parts we don't put ahead of God, that is—but rather trying to relive the past. Whenever I try, it never matches up to what I'm seeking. It only grows more elusive. It's become a painful thing to me for a reason. I believe God wants me to learn to live with the long view.

accept Christ a become part of eternity

There are two Greek words used in the Bible that both mean time: "chronos" which is time measured by an orbiting sun, or with a man's sundial, or with an imaginary rod; and "kairos" which is time measured by an eternity that transcends every moment but somehow connects them all. Chronos is quantifiable. Kairos is not subject to measure. Kairos pierced chronos when Jesus was born and when He died and when He resurrected. "For while we were still helpless, at the right time, Christ died for the ungodly" (Romans 5:6). That's kairos.

The day I accepted Christ (we'll get to that in good time), kairos pierced my heart. I didn't know it then, but I felt it as surely as I feel the heat from the sun's rays after they shoot across 93 million miles in eight minutes to reach me. And now as I write this, sitting on the back porch under the warmth of those rays, I'm reminded of that night when I was a young child staring out my bedroom window, connecting two stars and pondering infinity. I was at the intersection of chronos and kairos without realizing it. Amazingly, I can look out my window tonight and see those same two stars, though the one who saw them is gone. For I have a new spirit now, and a much older body. So be it. This body may have to trudge the earth in chronos, but my soul was made to ride in kairos forever.

Nothing in this life—past, present, or future—will be able to match up to the eternal reality I desire inside. That's the way it is. I can chase time till the sun burns down or accept time as it is and know that Jesus transcended it and therefore one day so will I. For now it's enough to know that God gives me, and all of us, enough time to accomplish what we're here to accomplish on any given day, just as surely as He gives each one of us enough of a lifetime to know His Son and accept Him as Savior.

Chapter 4

Into the Jungle

*Surely the most dangerous thing you can
do is to rationally vie with the devil;
after all, he is so capable in deceit.*

Michael Molinos

It took a while—two decades in fact—but I turned twenty. You'll notice I overshot my teen years by a convenient margin. The short version: I killed a lot of days bouncing tennis balls off the garage door, riding my bike through the shaded streets of South Miami, and waiting to grow into my answer. "Why am I here?" never left me. However, just as shrubs don't grow well in the shade, neither do lost souls who spend prodigal chunks of time in mischievous pursuits. Such were my teen years.

By now my venue had changed from Miami to Atlanta, and I believe that redirect salvaged my life. I was going to college, dating the woman I would marry, and living in a small apartment in the northern suburbs. Though my diversions waxed and waned, my drive to find the elusive meaning of my life was as strong as ever, and apparently it was perfectly happy running on minute traces of hope.

My philosophical bent, long weaned off Dr. Seuss and starter books, pored through the male rite-of-passage genre—*The Call of the Wild, The Adventures of Huckleberry Finn, Sherlock Holmes,* and the like; plowed through the requisite high school classics—*Great Expectations, The Scarlet Letter*, etc; and finally settled in with a pitcher of Kool-aid called self-help books.

With few exceptions (Dale Carnegie books come to mind), reading them was much like sugar overload after consuming a bagful of Halloween candy. I climbed and spiked with newfound direction, then crashed and burned when I realized their promised solutions were only a fleeting reprieve that led to another dead end. But I was obsessed with looking for answers and not to be deterred, and so wolfed down a zillion of those books, give or take. Only in later years could I look back and see that I should have just read *The Little Engine That Could*—"I think I can I think I can"—and saved a lot of time and money.

Nevertheless, I found these a good substitute for my college textbooks which for the most part were even more devoid of substance. And with growing recognition that the business curriculum I was on was wholly irrelevant to my cause, I chugged along through the college years mostly fine, indeed thinking I could, until I concluded from personal experience and with emphatic finality: I think I can't, I'm sure I can't, not anymore.

One day, shortly after graduation, I finally let go of my obsession with self-help books for good when I noticed that most of the souls in that section of the bookstore appeared the least stable of the lot. And I belonged right there with them. "I'm in big trouble," I thought more than once, continually actually.

The decade after college passed by in nothing flat—as in, a wink ago I was burning holes in leaves with my junior magnifying glass—and to my bewilderment I was now married, raising four children, and working in business. I found family life as satisfying as work was uninspiring, which is to say, I loved my family. On the whole, I did what you do: wade in head down, pretend to know what you're doing in life, and by all means put on a happy face. And there I plodded, lost as a goose.

By thirty I had moved on from the secular "be a better you" books, in a sideways direction I would say, and began reading a new genre—existentialist philosophy, dominated mostly by atheists, agnostics, and surely by retired college professors—which held forth the conviction that the individual determines his reality by his own thoughts and perceptions; in essence, there is no universal home base. That's called a free-for-all in my book and I was just desperate enough to believe it held some promise.

One particular version of existentialism delved into the world of quantum mechanics. If the big world didn't have any answers, perhaps the small one would. Philosophers pondered such perplexities as, "If a cat is in a box, is he only in there after you look inside?" To put it another way, did viewing the cat in effect cause it to be there?[4] ("You see officer, you viewed me to be speeding and that caused it to be so.") Or, "Light is both a wave and a particle at the same time, and it is we who cause one or the other to be actualized by virtue of our observation."[5] I'm oversimplifying these, but you get the common theme. Man determines reality. Right, and the actualized lemmings all follow.

I can perceive two plus two is five all day long but it won't make it so. That fails the most basic line of reasoning on several grounds, not the least of which is that none of my professors in my college days would ever agree my wrong test answers were merely their perceptions. Believe me, I tried that. I wasn't buying this brand of double-talk. I was quite certain that the cat and I were really here. It was why we were here that troubled me. Which is the very reason I chose to rummage further in the genre, next rubbing shoulders with the gloom found in books by Sartre, Kafka, and Nietzsche—giants of the faithless.[6]

Imagined conversation between Kafka and me:
Me: How ya doin' Franz?
Kafka: Pretty miserable.
Me: That's good.
Kafka: Yeah, I'm doing better.

I mean no disrespect to these smart men, and to atone for my sarcasm I feel obliged to offer this composite book review for their most influential contributions to society: moribund rudderless drivel. Childish, I know; I've always had a rebellious streak, particularly against self-refuting world views.

I finally came to my senses and abandoned this ship of lost hope, and promptly turned my attention to the great philosophers of antiquity, notably Socrates, Plato, and Aristotle. I learned much through their discourses, specifically the principals of logic. They were certainly out of my league but I sensed kindred souls from the start who enjoyed the process of thinking about thinking. Yet I had an end game. I never got the sense that they did. They'll be happy to know I still thought them rather admirable thinkers even though they pecked around most matters like a barnyard of confused chickens who swallow the shells and spit out the seeds. When it came to the question of ultimate meaning and why we are here, it didn't take long until I had a philosophical breakthrough: they were as lost as me.

So I concluded it was time to switch tracks again, and from man's books to man's religions I went, or did I writhe? Parallel desperations I should think. Any old religions would do, or half-baked new ones. I made a mental list of the most prominent ones and Christianity wasn't on the list. Neither was atheism. I couldn't stomach the thought. Most I quickly dismissed as not for me. For example, the thousand-gods view of Hinduism and its idea of potentially coming back as, say, an insect if I behaved poorly enough in this life didn't seem viable to me. How does one move up from insect? Once you've been demoted it seems impossible to reverse course. I mean, it's hard to earn your kudos when you spend your life eating other insects. So that religion was quickly dropped, as were several other *isms* due to comparable limitations.

The first one I really got immersed in was Buddhism, which I practiced for the better part of a year. I meditated for long hours yet could never quite get the hang of "losing myself" and being "one with the universe." I was too aware that my underlying goal was to find myself. In sum, I was a poor Buddhist. I briefly looked into other variations of "everything is God including me," pantheism as it's called. "But if I'm God I'm in big trouble," I thought, "and so is everyone else." Next.

Mormonism was quite appealing. I had a real sound reason for that though—I was a big Dale Murphy fan, number three, all-star outfielder for the Atlanta Braves. And if Mormonism was good enough for Murph, it was good enough for me. The problem, however, was that after reading *The Book of Mormon* and studying about the life of Joseph Smith, the religion's founder, I couldn't really see what Dale was seeing. The inconsistencies were fatal from the start: the universe has always existed; God was a man who was on another planet and then subsequently became a god who then created the universe and earth. Wait a minute! I thought the universe always existed. The problems grew worse the more I read. In the end I concluded Joseph Smith was a flawed man who made up his religion as he went along and Dale Murphy was a fine man who arguably should be in the Hall of Fame.

In my late twenties I was introduced to—read that, "suckered into"—Scientology. This was long before Hollywood made it fashionable. But I wasn't interested in trends; I was interested in truth. And evidently I was willing to go to desperate ends to find it. I quickly learned the objective in Scientology was to pursue what is called the state of "clear." I'm unclear how this works exactly, other than you pay lots of money for "auditing sessions" with someone who already paid enough themselves to in turn fleece the next willing dupe. To be audited meant you were brought back step by step to the earliest moments of your life, including those when you were still in the womb. You do all this, I'm told, to release the negative engrams in the brain. You follow?

I was assigned an auditor—an agreeable enough older man who apparently was at his post because he was out of ideas himself—who tried his best to train me to access my pre-birth thoughts. I believe he needed me to buy into what he was peddling so he could believe it himself. Were I to succeed as a compliant Scientologist, one day I would have been pronounced "clear," with the ultimate goal of realizing I'm a thetan which, as I was to find out much later, would have allowed me to connect with the outer space alien (singular intended) who colonized our planet sixty thousand years ago. Honest! I mean, absurd! But that's what they believe. I eventually got to the point that I was no longer intrigued, just in awe of their brashness and deception. Maybe I'm being too tough on Scientology. After all, it's founder, L. Ron Hubbard, was a crackerjack science fiction writer.

Science fiction notwithstanding, I got out of that religion as fast as I got in—one day literally race-walking out of the building and to my car once I knew it was really over.

Not many months after my walking escape to freedom, I drove past a small house set back in a serene wooded setting. The sign out front read, "Transcendental Meditation Center." Sure, why not? I turned down the driveway for what became the first of many times. Early on I received my mantra which is only given by the teacher to star students and after you pay money. Only the qualified can tell which is your mantra, you see. I spent hours meditating while chanting that mantra next to a trickling fountain for background. To this day I keep hoping to forget it. I believe it is the name of a demon. Turns out I was never able to "transcend my body" like the masters supposedly could, unless you count falling asleep. That fact along with the pressure to buy their purification food-paste and special oils to anoint my body—I'm a soap guy—and I knew it was time to move on again. I found out years later that had I stayed with it longer I would have learned to levitate and become invisible. So apparently I left right before the good stuff.

I never bought into any of these religions, mind you. Rather I sought to disprove them, while simultaneously hoping at least one would have my answer. It was mostly a process of elimination. To me, all the major religions existed on a giant decision tree: if yes, proceed ahead, if no, exit stage right. And while I didn't become an expert in these, I didn't merely dabble in them either. I researched and studied them, and as soon as I saw one as false, I moved on to the next one, until after a while I noticed a pattern—not one religion held up to scrutiny, not even close. I was running out of exits and fast becoming an inwardly disillusioned sort. Why am I here? Beats the pajamas off me. Had I known the book of Ecclesiastes back then, I would have "Amen-ed" where Solomon writes, "I have seen all the things that are done under the sun; all of them are meaningless, a chasing after the wind" (1:14, NIV). I needed the wind to smack me in the face quick.

It's sad that so many are deceived by man-made religions. When you look them over carefully you wonder how all these people could be so taken in. Then you read that this is nothing new:

"Professing to be wise, they became fools, and exchanged the glory of the incorruptible God for an image in the form of corruptible man and of birds and four-footed animals and crawling creatures....For they exchanged the truth of God for a lie, and worshiped and served the creature rather than the Creator, who is blessed forever. Amen" (Romans 1:22, 23, 25).

They looked everywhere God wasn't—on purpose!—and they became fools.

Speaking as one, as I said, Christianity wasn't a branch of my decision tree and I was flat out of ideas. Which is it? A thousand gods? We're all gods? God is from outer space and so am I? Untenable all. I was left with three options: atheism—unacceptable to every fiber of my soul and easily dismissed if intellectual honesty is of concern; some yet-to-be discovered *ism* that for the life of me or anyone else we can't seem to figure out; or the theism taught throughout the Western world—there is one God Who created it all and I'm not Him. Nah, that's not it. Too easy. So there I sat in a tree of religions, out of branches to explore, which soon led to the troublesome thought that I might not live long enough to find my answer.

Chapter 5

THE RÉSUMÉ

Go in the strength you have.

GOD TO GIDEON

I would never want you to think I was pandering to you, my dear, favorite reader, but I suddenly realized we've come this far and I have yet to avail you of my many qualifications to write about such a matter as a journey into the heart of God. Perhaps an academic and professional biography of my credentials are in order.

First some background: I was accepted to seminary twice, but never completed the process. The first time, God halted the proceedings when I heard Him say, "Are you getting this degree for Me, for you, or for them?"

"Um, don't I need a degree to, you know, do ministry things?"

"What do you think, son?"

Some choices aren't black or white, right or wrong, but are red or blue, like picking out a new bike. At that moment I sensed God wanted me to decide with my heart. So I chose a blue one. Many friends I know chose red and earned prestigious seminary degrees which they employ with great faith, integrity, and to the benefit of many. I wasn't so led. I'm prone to getting caught up in the weeds of knowledge and missing the heart. I believe God wanted me to find mine and start leading with it.

Nevertheless, "Knowledge puffs up" (1 Corinthians 8:1, NIV), and for the wrong reasons, a few years later I revisited the idea of going to seminary.

"Yes, God, but think how much good I can do with all those letters and honorable titles after my name."

"How about "Kevin, Fisherman" as a title?" He suggested.

I liked that and began casting.

Now without further ado, I present the life-shaping highlights and lowlights which led me to believe I was qualified to write this book:

Kindergarten: I failed at blocks. The manual dexterity needed to make a credible stack proved too difficult to master. Unless I'm called to build storehouses for grain like Joseph in the land of Egypt, this shouldn't disqualify me, although it does preclude making a decent living in the craftsmen trades. Still and all, kindergarten was the academic highlight of my life. I aced everything else, did all my dot-to-dots, excelled at nap time, and warbled "E-I-E-I-O" with the best of them. But none of that compared to the books.

On the very first week I was called upon to read out loud from a book in the Dick and Jane series about the children's visit to their grandparents' farm.[7] I bedazzled all within earshot, I'm sure, and a lifelong romance with books (and farms) began. I had been reading books at home for as long as I could remember, which was about two years, but this was the seminal book that launched me forth into the captivating world of words. And so with confidence brimming, as quick as you can say "Doctor of Philosophy Kindergarten," I was on my way to big boy school, already substantially formed for better or worse into the personality I would have for the rest of my life.

Elementary School: In grade school where life is a sheltered cakewalk, the personality still finds ways to stray. In my case, unbeknownst to me, I ran afoul of the Bible by using words in a sinful manner: I swore oaths ("Cross my heart, hope to die, stick a needle in my eye"), refused to turn the other cheek ("I'm rubber, you're glue, anything you say bounces off of me and sticks to you"), then redeemed myself somewhat by learning to parry like a Socratic master ("Sticks and stones may break my bones but words will never hurt me"), but, alas, sadly relapsed when I became the reigning cussing champion of my block three years running, with consequence I might add. Washing one's mouth out with soap is the expression.

And so in the end these elementary years taught me the invaluable lesson of repentance, something I continued to learn for several decades before actually getting around to doing it.

For the most part, I was a walking dichotomy: melancholy and carefree; bookworm studious and Three Stooges silly; relational and introspective; well-adjusted and unsure of my place in the big wide romper room of life. However, there was one area in which I was not at all dichotomous. To the contrary, I was as single-mindedly consistent as sunrise. Every day I walked home from school lost in my thoughts and kicking an empty soda can the whole way. I mused and amused my way through six years of elementary school, miles of steps and hundreds of cans, my soul matching each clank with an unspoken, yet clattering, "Help, help, help…"

"Seek, and you will find," the Scriptures say (Matthew 7:7). We shall see.

Junior High: If ever there were a place to not find the why of life, it was at junior high during the me-me 70s. I attended a public school that borrowed heavily from Alcatraz, I'm thinking. I use the term "school" loosely here, for this one sported as bankrupt a curriculum as you'll ever find. The academic nadir was the English class called "Modern Rock Poetry" that my brother had to take. I missed that one, but instead was required to take part in a regrettable new math course where the numbers didn't have to add up—not overly inspiring for one with truth-seeking inclinations.

I spent three years scurrying through halls of bureaucratic mediocrity with an armful of textbooks whose pages had begun melding together from inactivity. Though to be fair, maybe I learned more than I thought. As they say, the sculptor takes away everything in the slab not part of the work till what remains is the vision.

My vision back then was this: pretend I was tough (not fisticuffs so much as a facial expression thing all guys learn), act unbefuddled in the presence of all those beguiling females, and fake my way through the most apathy-inducing so-called modern curriculum ever devised—up until then anyway. It was your standard-issue test of survival, and should you ever want all your foundations shaken to the core, I highly recommend it.

Junior high shook mine. Peer-pressure dictated social modalities, and my philosophical outbursts were not among the accepted norms. All was not lost. I did find time to play sports, chase girls, have a healthy dose of friends in the neighborhood, and successfully negotiate the hallways of bullies worse off than me, pretending all the while that I wasn't out of my element, which of course I was. I wasn't the guy who got hung on a hook in the gym locker room, but I wasn't class president material either.

The highlight of those three years came after a football game. I noticed a girl from my school sitting on the bleachers all by her lonesome, and since she was pretty, I thought it worth my while to talk with her. She surprised me, however, when she steered the conversation right away to the subject of God, inquiring whether I believed in Him or not. I can't recall my responses, but I'm sure they were of the fumbling kind. She spent the next twenty minutes telling me about her faith in Jesus, and I am certain my soul was trembling.

I listened, fully rapt, and felt myself being drawn to what she was saying. But unfortunately it was not to be that day. It was just too foreign to what I had been exposed to, plus I didn't quite get it when she said all I had to do was believe Jesus is Savior and I would go to Heaven. I liked the idea of it but it didn't reach to the depths of my soul. In retrospect, maybe that was because she spoke nothing about repentance or receiving Christ (after all, even devils believe He exists), or if she did, I missed it that day, and for many more to come.

High School: If the bar was set in junior high at how to make it through the day without tripping up the stairs, the expectations in high school were raised almost a full tad. My father, an attorney and accountant by training, accepted a well-paying job as a partner of a national accounting firm in Atlanta, Georgia. And so just two months prior to the start of school, I left the land of scampering lizards and casual climes for one of emerald magnolias and old Southern charm.

The adjustment forced me to grow up, mostly the awkward hard way, which meant I learned to keep my feelings as tightly packed as the Georgia red clay. No matter. Kids cope, and I did so by seizing the chance to reinvent myself. I tried a few roles on for size—the strong, silent type, á la actor Clint Eastwood; or maybe an affable *Smokey and the Bandit* Burt Reynolds; and when all else failed I tried a composite of them both with a bit of old-school

James Dean brooding thrown in for good measure. I couldn't pull off any of those so in the end I settled on me, who I hid remarkably well.

My father was climbing the overrated ladder of success, my mom was busy with my dad, my brother was away at college, and I was a spiritually impoverished mess. I can't recall a single encounter with God or anyone who talked about God in those years. I used the time to develop a few more social skills, which really means I got better at pretending I had them. "Why am I here?" got overtaken by an all-out effort to personify some group ideal of coolness and right behavior. This is how you wear your hair, this is how you nonchalantly flip your hair to the side, this is how you flip your hair while simultaneously holding your books in the grip of your hand and not in your arms like a girl. Admittedly that last bit was good to know.

On the inside, the philosopher in me turned out the lights, and took a three-year nap. Such was high school. I remember vividly that dread in the pit of my stomach before school each day, like an actor's opening night jitters before a live audience. Every day felt like that to me, and I was constantly working on my fallback role—nonpareil chameleon. Teenage peer pressure is unrelenting and I survived it in large part by never losing sight of the fact that I wasn't really like this. Not that I had any clue who the real me was, nor did anyone else made of flesh and blood.

How does high school qualify someone with a bad case of soul amnesia to speak of his journey into the heart of God? Simple. I know firsthand what it feels like to be sad beyond measure, profoundly confused, and gravely lost, and yet to one day be found.

<u>College</u>: After graduation I was still exploring Atlanta, so instead of wandering aimlessly around some far away bucolic campus, I chose to stay lost at a local bricks and mortar city college. It was a let down. I hear from so many people who look back on their college days with great fondness. I had high hopes for mine but they were never reached.

Early on in college I had a dream that a big wind picked me up and whooshed me up to a cloud where I sat and was able to look down at my home. Then I panned across and saw the continents of the world much like on a globe. As soon as my eyes fixed on Africa, a fierce gust knocked me off the cloud and I fell all the way into a shallow lagoon in the center of the continent. *Splash!* Fortunately I was unhurt. I slowly looked around at the surrounding lush foliage and heard the unmistakable jungle sounds of monkeys, lions, and exotic birds. As I began to crawl the few feet to dry land, I put my hand on the ground and a poisonous snake bit me and I died. Some will tell me there is a Freudian meaning packed into that dream, but I have boiled it down to its essence: all my options stink, including the upcoming midterms.

I was still trying to fit in, but not so much with my peers anymore—funny how one year in the wider world softens that focus. In this case, I wanted to fit in to something I knew my father valued—success in business. I was proud of his success, and since I had always pursued his approval, I chose a business major hoping it was a shortcut.

I sleepwalked through all the customary classes on accounting basics and management principals, and came to consciousness whenever I walked past the liberal arts part of the college. I would read the words displayed on the doors: Department of Psychology, Sociology, Archaeology, Anthropology, Any-ology. Quite simply my heart ached to study an "ology" (which is redundant, you know?). But it never happened. At the time I just couldn't outrun my desire for paternal affirmation, not that any of us do; though in retrospect I do see God's hand in keeping me safe from the secular ideologies contained in many liberal arts pursuits. There is saving grace in a business degree that requires minimal deprogramming.

Yoked to my business studies and bored out of my skull, I went to the bookstores in my free time where I immersed myself in assorted subjects that masked the real cry in my heart, and waited for the four years to be over, which they were in five thanks to my time-consuming minor of 101 Ways to Kick a Can Down the Road in Your Mind. And in spite of my least efforts, I survived the ordeal and was given a degree in business anyway.

To celebrate, I went out and bought a puppy that I named Noah.

The Business Years: I emerged from my educational purgatory feeling much like a disoriented tourist emerging from the jungle after a trip gone horribly wrong—in other words, feeling exactly like my college dream—and promptly entered the business world.

Age ≈ 55

It was 1984. Look at me, world. Look at me, Dad. Just like you. Only you seem so contented and I haven't a clue. I didn't get into lawyering or accounting. Those were his passions; mine were philosophizing and ruminating. And as I hadn't the guts to grow a long beard and walk through hill and dale in a white robe, after a careful process of elimination—all structured jobs were out, all non-business jobs simply had to be out—I fell into the last job standing: a commercial real estate position in booming Atlanta, Georgia. It was a good direction to fall. The environment gave me indispensable freedom, financial upside (100 percent commissioned positions are all upside!), and a place to interact with a cross section of smart-like people.

By the early 90s, a close friend—a former competitor in the same business—and I had formed our own company. The business, our friendship, and our respective families grew over what proved to be reliable years, and as a bonus, the responsibilities of life kept my head down and out of the clouds half the time. The other half, my business partner got to hear every nuance of philosophical thought I was compelled to parse. Day after day, year after year, he listened beyond what any friend should have to. Together we sharpened each other, the culmination being that we both came to the same conclusion in the same year: there is ultimate meaning to life and His name is Jesus (and now I am ahead of my own story again).

Ministry and Today: The decision to give my life to Jesus proved to be my business downfall. After a long career of being a businessman outwardly (turns out I got more enjoyment retelling my dad's successful business story than I ever got by living my own), I began hearing the call on the inside to full-time ministry. I was rough around the edges in my faith but full-bore in my enthusiasm for God. Still, I resisted the urge to jump into ministry, settling for putting my toe in the water by leading Bible study groups and the like.

The year after I accepted Christ, I told a man who had embarked on ministry decades before that I kind of fancied leaving real estate and doing what he does. His three-word response dampened my eagerness and was not picked up by motivational speakers or sporting goods pitchmen: "Don't do it." Then he added, "People who come to Christ understandably get excited and sometimes think they should pursue vocational ministry when in fact they can usually best do ministry from the perch of their current job." I thought it well-intentioned, good advice for most, but well-intentioned, bad advice for me. But God can use any advice and turn it to His advantage, which He did by sanding me down over the next fifteen years as I stayed put.

I was brought to the precipice of vocational ministry again years later when one too many times I was sitting in a business meeting hitting someone over the head with my favorite subject, the meaning of life, while my business partner was trying to get some work done that would pay to keep the lights on, or something similarly unimportant. At one point the client interrupted me. "I thought you guys were going to share some helpful insights about our real estate," he said. Since I didn't have any, I decided right then and there that I had to move on with my life. A few months later, I worked up the courage to follow my heart and I entered full-time vocational ministry, which soon led to the writing of this book, and all in full disobedience of the man who had advised me to stay out of it.

And there you have it, the full unvarnished truth—not counting the varnished parts—and my qualifications to write this book.

—⟶⟶⟶—

I had the occasion recently to meet with the pastor of a large church to talk about the vocation of ministry in general. I'd never met him before. So before we got started he said he'd like to learn more about me and the ministry, then asked if I would bear with him while he asked a few questions. I wasn't sure where he was going, but said something like, "Sure, sounds like fun." What followed amounted to an examination: "What are your views on ecclesiology? How about soteriology? Eschatology? The sacraments? And by the way, where did you go to seminary?"

I was disappointed beyond belief, or rather because of my belief. Once I would have jumped at the chance to discuss all the *ologies* I could. But there's a time and place and this wasn't it, not after a lifetime of leading with my head and then finally realizing God was leading me on a journey of the heart. I answered the man's questions, presumably passed, and we moved on, but later that night I reflected back on what he didn't say: "Tell me about your journey of faith. How is your relationship with God today? Isn't Jesus wonderful? In what ways does Jesus make your socks go up and down? How did He speak to you in His Word today? What is the latest answer to prayer you've received?" The questions didn't stop until I fell asleep.

To espouse head knowledge might have the appearance of godliness, but without connecting it to the heart, we risk becoming spiritual bogs, or worse, spiritual bullies. I believe he was a good man, my brother in Christ at that, but that didn't stop me from being irritated. I could see too much of me in him not to be.

Too often I'm prone to forget that "Christ in you, the hope of glory" (Colossians 1:27) is my only necessary qualification to spread the good news, to share my story. Not Christ plus a degree, or Christ plus how many verses I've memorized, or Christ plus anything else. Jesus Christ alone. Imagine being told by someone you should only speak English if you have an English degree. Preposterous! We all speak Bible if we're God's children, and I bristle when anyone implies we don't. We are all fishermen, are we not?

There is an expression I've heard more than once, that God doesn't call the qualified; He qualifies the called. It took a while for me to come to the end of myself, to where I could no longer deny that God was calling me to full-time vocational ministry. I held on to the ledge of self-direction with the last might of my fingernails until, mercifully, I had no choice but to let go, and found to my surprise I had been one inch off the ground all along. And having relinquished my grip, naively convinced the hard part was now behind me, I walked from the comfort of an easy routine and a regular paycheck into the biggest adventure of my life.

I suppose the road could have been easier, certainly shorter, but that wouldn't have been better, for I don't think I would have learned that although I chose God, first and foremost He chose me. And that is the ultimate qualification, don't you think? It also winds us back, in a convenient sort of way, to my early premise that God in His kindness chose to make me so I could enter into the heart of Jesus. How exactly did I do that? I'm glad you asked.

Chapter 6

PURSUING THE LION

Ah, but a man's reach should exceed his grasp,
Or what's a heaven for?

ROBERT BROWNING

After years of consuming mind-numbing quantities of self-help books and trying on for size a healthy assortment of religions of the world (minus one), by my early thirties, I was left with a growing ache in my soul and a robust cynicism. Yet even though my coping strategies were wearing thin, I was not ready to throw in the towel. I well knew that this was life or death for my heart.

One day I was soothing my pain through mindless television fare, when I saw an ad for a publishing company that promised to expand my horizons through reading "the one hundred greatest books ever written"—books such as *Moby Dick, Don Quixote, The Brothers Karamazov, A Tale Of Two Cities,* and so on. The books were advertised as handsome, leather-bound editions with gold inlay lettering, masterpieces guaranteed to make you look smart just by putting them on your shelf. For a mere thirty-seven dollars apiece you would receive one per month and could cancel anytime with no penalty. They certainly seemed weightier nourishment than the books I had been reading. Count me in.

And just like that I was immersed once again in the comforting world of books. The best news of all was that when the first book of the series arrived, the package contained a list of the remaining books that would be sent each month. I canceled faster than you can say "overbearing infomercial," then promptly rushed down to the local bookstore and discovered, most agreeably, that the cheapest books of all are the classics. The better the book the cheaper the price.

I filled my bookshelves at home and spent the better part of five years reading through the incomparable Western literature classics, reading every word of every book. It was one of the best things I ever did. Along with great writing, eye-opening history, and captivating plots, it turns out that most of these classics had an underlying theme that previous generations in the West must have appreciated—there is a God, and therefore there is a point to life, a morality not made by man, but discoverable by him. And as I read through each of these books, over the walk of time their stories began to incline my heart a certain way.

By 1992, I was barreling through my reading marathon and renting space for my one-man eponymous real estate business at a small office park in suburban Atlanta (I hadn't yet met my future friend and business partner). The tenant next door was a small company whose owner was a pleasant enough man who I never took the time to get to know. We'd pass each other in the parking lot and wave or nod. The few times we did talk, I didn't find him to be a riveting conversationalist, or overly interesting, or outwardly sharp. To this day, I can't remember his name. I suppose I can't rule out that he was an angel.

One late afternoon as I walked to my car to head home for the weekend, he waved me down to ask if I wanted to come to a men's Bible study that evening.

I tried to be polite. "No thanks. That's really not my thing."

He persisted, "What do you think about the Bible anyway?"

Game on. "I think it's a good book with solid moral values, but not *the* Word of God by any means," I informed him. "Just a good book by smart men."

He looked at me peaceably and smiled. "Well let me know if you change your mind." Then he left (angel for sure).

I stood there for five minutes in cold silence feeling like a little boy who just got caught with his hand in the cookie jar. Here's this rather unassuming guy that I had no real connection with, and he invites me to a Bible study, and now I'm left standing there thinking, "Isn't this funny. I'm all puffed up about reading the so-called 'one hundred greatest books ever written,' and the Bible isn't even on the list." Although I'd never read the Bible, somehow that wasn't palatable. So I went home and decided—in the interest of scholarly thoroughness, mind you—to track one down and read it.

I was surprised to find one with an inscription from my Aunt Joy and Uncle Jack, dated Christmas, 1969, stuffed way back in the closet with the aforementioned scorpions from childhood. I never read it in those days, but I did suddenly remember that I used to be fascinated by the cover—a color depiction of Adam and Eve running through a beautiful garden, un-garbed but for scanty leaves, and looking quite anxious.

Over the next several months, I read that Bible cover to cover, every name in Genesis, every lamentation, psalm, and abstract symbolism in Revelation. I'm sure I even read the publisher's preface. Not that I understood much of what I read, but when I was done I could sense my heart was stirring just a little more. I had a sense I was on the trail of something big, but didn't know yet that I was pursuing a Lion.

Adding to this convergence of influences, on my long drives to and from work I happened upon a regular radio show featuring Ravi Zacharias, a gifted speaker and skilled Christian apologist whom I took to instantly.[8] Inspiration struck early on and I turned my attention to the subject of apologetics, the logical defense of the Christian faith, adding another genre to my reading list and filling my head with promising and novel ideas.

The more I read, the more compelling the subject became, though I was always careful to temper my enthusiasm with a rather surprising filter in my brain. It said, "Would Dad be convinced by this?" Certain points sure convinced me, such as the brilliant treatise in C.S. Lewis's *Mere Christianity* on how morality speaks of a transcendent and loving God; Thomas Aquinas's *Summa*

Theologica and his proofs that there must be only one God and not many as the Greeks supposed; and Pascal's *Pensées*, where oddly enough his simple comment "Man is a thinking reed" hit the mark with me.[9] Indeed, what other creature admires the beauty in cloud formations and finds in their forms the shapes of a whale, a ship, or Winston Churchill? Neither a dolphin nor Koko the sign language gorilla can do such a thing. Eureka! Man *is* a thinking reed! Not mere matter, or another part of nature, but something more. Animals think. Man thinks deeply, abstractly. Man asks, "Why am I here?"

—⁂—

One day I pulled my head away from a book long enough to accept a lunch invitation from a friend who wanted me to meet his friend, Dr. Ken Boa, a well-respected speaker, teacher, and writer.[10] "You'll enjoy the discussions," he said." Ken goes deep." I was not disappointed. He talked deeply all right, while I listened intently to his words about everything from distant stars and big bangs to transcendent meaning and a personal God. I left thinking I may have just met the smartest man I'll ever meet.

Soon after, I began attending a monthly men's group with Ken and four or five other bright, warmhearted men. We'd meet for lunch and have a sort of round table discussion in an authentic fellowship I was not accustomed to or comfortable with. I was the agnostic among these thoughtful Christians and so, while Ken led, I tried to take on the role of antagonist to the group. "Yeah but... yeah but..." But for every "yeah but," it turned out that Ken and company always had answers, intellectually appealing ones at that. For the first time I was included in a group of people who lived life with the full understanding that it had true meaning.

Though I was fighting a losing battle, still I fought. A soul being led to face his Maker strides in manfully with dignity to lay down his pride, or he goes in heels first, digging a rut the whole long way. My pride burrowed, but God kept loving me anyway. He had me surrounded.

With my options for escape dimming, it was about this time that Tony, a friend from my early real estate days, returned from New York University where he'd been for the past year to earn his master's degree. I'd known Tony a long time and when he came back from school he was a markedly different man. I asked him what had changed and he recounted how his Christian girlfriend had influenced him to return to the faith of his childhood. Turns out, unbeknownst to me, he was raised in a Christian home and had accepted Christ at a young age. And here I thought he was just my beer-drinking friend.

I was intrigued by Tony's renewed faith, and frequently over the next six months, we had a spirited, ongoing dialogue about such topics as, "Is there a God?" "Is Jesus the Son of God?" and, "Is the Bible accurate?" I knew where he was leading me. That's where I was hoping to get. But I wasn't going unless I was fully convinced.

I admire people who jump with simple faith, but I needed to know what the parachute was made of, how it was packed, and the laws of aerodynamics before I jumped.

I recall Tony saying something to the effect of, "You go for that apologetic, head stuff. That's not my thing. But it is my pastor's thing, and if you're up for it, he's already offered to meet with you on a regular basis to work through any questions you have." Tag-teaming me, were they? Bring it on, fellas.

I met with his pastor who stated the ground rules in our first meeting: keep an open mind and use logic. Logic—my middle name. The meetings with the pastor were going well, but over time, I think I must have worn him down, not because he wasn't right about Jesus being the Savior of the world (as I learned later he was—and He is), but because my will wasn't right. I could always come up with another objection, and no amount of talking was moving me over that line. Logic is no match for stubborn will. Our discussions ran their course and after a few meetings more I stopped hearing from the pastor, and then I stopped hearing from Tony as well.

On a crisp October day in 1996, I called Tony from my car to find out why he no longer approached me to talk about the subject of God.

"I'm out of ammo," he responded, "and there's nothing more I know to say."

"So that's it? You're done with me?" It took several more minutes of my prying before he reluctantly shared the most disarming words I'd ever heard.

"No, it's not that. A friend and I have made a pact to call each other once a week to pray for you. That's all."

"You what?" I heard him, but had to compose myself. "That's a bit out of the ordinary, don't you think? Two grown men don't have anything better to do than pray for me? Shouldn't you be talking about last night's ball game or some such thing?"

My amiable friend chuckled.

I squirmed. No one had ever told me that they were praying for me before. I simply had no category for it, and no defense. I remember after I hung up feeling like an arrow had pierced my heart, which it had, and of having the sensation of being intellectually and emotionally spent. As I sat in my car and mulled over every angle of why these two men would do something so selfless, I came up with no viable answer, other than—dare I think it, a word that back then I didn't associate with a male friend—love. I drove home in a mental daze (benumbed is the word), fully aware that there was no more thinking to do, no other books to read, no knowledge left to consider.

Faith. It's similar to belief but it's more. You can believe something but still not act on that belief. I had sufficient head knowledge, but no faith. Faith acts. I can know that there's a chair in the corner of the room with four sturdy legs. I can believe that it would hold me up if I decided to sit down. But faith is an act of the will. It's what puts me in that chair. As I drove along, I had a private conversation in my head. "I know that Jesus has my best interests at heart, and that I can trust Him. But am I willing to give Him my heart? I believe that I am."

The Bible says, "Ask and it will be given to you" (I had been doing that since I was five), "seek and you will find" (for as long as I can remember), and "knock and the door will be opened to you" (Matthew 7:7, NIV). That night, in the unceremonious surrounds of my own bathroom, I knocked. I got on my knees and prayed for God's forgiveness and for Jesus to come into my life, and He did. The Lion roared.

Part Two

THE LOVERS

Chapter 7

MEANING, MORALITY, AND G.K.

All things came into being through Him,
and apart from Him nothing came into
being that has come into being.

JOHN 1:3

When I came to know Jesus, in an instant I knew why I was here. The point of everything in my life up to then was to find my answer. Now I had it and began experiencing a peace and purpose I'd never felt before. I knew that I would be with God and live forever and that life would never be meaningless again. Truth be told, it is meaningless to say life is meaningless anyway (and right now some are thinking that sentence is meaningless). That we strange creatures ponder the matter at all hints at something beyond ourselves. A frog on a lily pad never ponders. He only waits to see his fly. But man knows there is more than meets the eye (rhyme unintended, but I'll take it). Even to the atheists among us, who like to pretend otherwise, meaning is an actual thing or else they wouldn't bother stopping at red lights.

Growing up, I searched for that meaning amidst all the creature comforts one ever needs. But "all" is a relative term when you find the whole world isn't enough. Observing the so-called Protestant work ethic of my parents certainly didn't add to my concept of ultimate meaning in life. I only internalized earth-bound ethics like, "The early bird gets the worm," and, "Keep your nose to the grindstone."

My parents were a proud product of their generation: depression-era babies, born in the soul-mooring days of necessity when "duty first" was alive and well. Work hard, make no excuses, and get on with it. Even the wide-eyed idealism of Walt Disney bowed to the adage of the times: "You gotta work to get along."[11] It was true, of course. Dad concurred. Mom too, with her attitude of "Use common sense, and don't rest till you've taken take care of your family and your home, or die trying." There was love in all of it, and I know now why my parents worked as hard as they did. But back then, through the seeking eyes of a boy, I missed Jesus in that work ethic. I couldn't see the meaning in it. Nor in its counterpart, "Let us eat and drink, for tomorrow we may die"(Isaiah 22:13). That is not a winning proposition. The tomorrow we die stuff is kind of a problem. That was my sense as a boy, and it has to be the logical conclusion of anyone who is honest enough to think it through today.

I can while away an hour watching ants move great mounds speck by speck. They are impressive workers, but I'm quite sure they don't know why they're doing it. When I'm outside I can feel the wind doing its job moving the clouds and spreading the pollen. "Round and round it goes..." (Ecclesiastes 1:6, NIV) unaware I am here. Meaning cannot come from creatures or forces of nature. How could it? Both exist inside a closed system, as do you and I. This entire universe—vast and lively—is closed. Thus if there is to be meaning in any real sense, it must be infused transcendentally; it must enter from the outside. All men can see for themselves that stars shine, rains fall, flowers grow, and people laugh and then they die. But only some men ask, "Is there an outside? And if so, where is the opening to get there?"

For me that opening appeared on that October day through the prayers of two friends. And it only got wider in the days ahead as I doubled my reading and zeroed in on my latest favorite subject, apologetics—a truth-seeker's dream and an atheist's nightmare. The Bible, I quickly learned, is the greatest apologetic work, and I spent much time there, in the source book of creation as it were. "Where were you when I laid the foundations of the earth?" God asks Job (Job 38:4). Indeed where were any of us?

I was particularly drawn to the works and words of the brilliant philosopher and apologist Dr. William Lane Craig, who taught such principles as the *kalam* cosmological argument: "The beginning of the universe points to a creator. For whatever begins to exist has a cause (name one material thing that doesn't); the universe began to exist; therefore, the universe has a cause."[12]

→ God

Some would shout out a last-ditch salvo that perhaps space and time go back in an infinite regress. But in point of logic, if that were the case, they would never have arrived here to lodge their protest. You can't span infinite time and get to the present. Try to wriggle out as we may, there is no other explanation. Only a Being Who transcends both space and time could choose to begin this closed system. Seems like I've read these truths somewhere before: "In the beginning, God...."

Some through guile like to promote a different beginning, and for the longest time they fooled me. On a coffee table in the living room of my childhood home was a hardcover book by the publishers of *Life* magazine. Inside its pages purported to be the account of how mankind got here on Earth, and I believed it. Six color sketches told the story of a monkey morphing over millions of years to become a man. Today, in the interest of self-preservation, the so-called experts have gotten more elaborate in their fabrication, but the message is every bit as cold and deceptive—we evolved.[13]

By the time I went to college, the institutions and media had coordinated their assault to convince me just how that happened— an impersonal universe forced itself onto the scene from out of the midst of nothingness (the fatal problem that nothingness has no midst hadn't yet occurred to me). This they called the big bang— an explosion that produced gases and particles that accreted into clumps of pre-planets and pre-stars, giving birth to our solar system, the earth, the oceans, amoebas, and oft-mentioned mudfish, one of which crawled onto shore. And that's how we got people and cats. The end. As my mind adapted to that guileful story, indeed my heart came to its end. A scientist makes a poor philosopher when he insists on using only the tools of science to explain transcendent matters. How many beakers of love does it take to fill the human heart? What is the square root of hope? Which chemicals can you mix in a Bunsen burner to find meaning?

There can be no meaning in molecules.

—◊◊◊—

"What is truth?" a scoffer once asked Jesus (John 18:38). How disingenuous. We all know the answer: Truth is that which corresponds to reality and is why my hand hurts when I put it over a flame. These days truth itself, though invincible, is increasingly under assault. But what point is there in pretending non-reality? It doesn't exist. Even as a nonbeliever I got that. Though prior to accepting Jesus, I did spend several wasteful years putting my hopes in reality-denying notions like parallel universes (apparently I was bored with the perpendicular kind), Eastern religions (why aren't there north and south ones?), or Atlanta Falcon playoff victories.[14]

"They sow the wind and reap the whirlwind" (8:7, NIV) warned the prophet Hosea regarding wayward Israel. We are in the process of finding out what that feels like. Increasingly, those who scoff at truth in our society have gone over to a more aggressive form of anti-God zealotry, notably in the guise of the relativists and their cousins the nihilists. They patrol reality looking for any way to bring it down. The relativists believe in everything except for objective truth and morality, as in two plus two equals anything you want. The nihilists deny everything and believe nothing matters, as in two plus two equals zero. I've never met a practicing nihilist to my knowledge and don't think they exist other than in the constructs of deluded minds.

Nonexistent conversation:
Nihilist: I believe in nothing.
Me: Belief is not nothing and neither is I. Thus you're either a figment or you're a phony nihilist.
Nihilist: …

Assuming they aren't figments, then these people are really apathetic relativists who like to play make-believe that nothing matters. It's their way of disengaging from a pursuing God. Of course the stratagem of the relativists is equally fatal:

Relativist: There is no such thing as absolute truth.
Me: Is that true?
Relativist: Absolutely!

They sink unawares, holding the rock they claim doesn't exist—*blub, blub, blub.*
So to sum it all up, the nihilists are actually relativists who in turn are absolutists who like to pretend everything is relative so they

don't have to respond to a truth-demanding God. Straightforward enough.

There's an old wry joke about a lost visitor who drives into a small town, pulls up to a man at the gas station, and asks for directions to the Johnsons' farm. "You can't get there from here," the man says. Well, I finally see what that man means. To both the relativists and the nihilists I say, "I can't get there from here." I spent years lost in that God-denying nonsense and I won't go back. Truth is not whatever we choose to make it. It is something we discover when our hearts are ready.

The sharp-witted English writer G.K. Chesterton is often credited with originating the saying, "When people don't believe in God, they don't believe in nothing, they believe in everything."[15] Eloquent, pithy, true. For the relativists, nihilists, and all those who whistle past the graveyard holding spirits at bay who don't exist, I believe their illogical thinking originates in a will that says, "I refuse. I refuse to admit to objective truth because if I do, I'll have to admit to a Truth-giver, and I'd rather believe He's not there so I can live my life of self-indulgence. Therefore, there are multiple truths, including my own, so I'll thank you to leave me alone now and let me live my life on my terms."

It's a heart issue, not a logic one.

I wish in the heat of the moment I were a man of noble discourse like G.K. Chesterton—one who could easily and calmly respond to the relativists' self-serving blather. But too often all my emotions scream and pout like a spoiled child when I'm riled by a moral relativist. I want to respond in love but I also want to fiercely defend what I love. I hope to do better. For anyone who challenges me on the matter in the future, I have a dream that I'll do it all the right way one day. A dream that I'll respond in the heart of the moment.

"Yes, my friend," I would say. "There is truth. It's true that I love dogwood trees. It's true that I hate long lines. It's true that there is love, that poignant movies make me cry, and that I try to pretend they don't. It's true that there is pain and suffering. It's true that I don't like cats much and that inexplicably I have two. It's true that there is redemption and that repentance leads to peace. It's true that even relativists look both ways before crossing the street. It's true that there is good and evil. It's true that two plus two equals four and never five. It's also true that God is love and that He loves you. Truth isn't dry, my friend. It is the most romantic thing in the world. Truth is the character of God. And when we ignore that little detail, truth comes calling with sobering results—separation from God and all that that entails. It's true that you have a chance to change that now. It's true that God loves you that much." *Poof.* Awake.

I'm hopelessly unpersuadable. There is nothing of value I can ever know apart from God and His truth. I dared to dream for that back before I knew Him, though I didn't have a name to give to that dream. Then, in the first moments after I turned to Christ, my soul rewound my life's quest and I had an inward conversation:

Mind: So life is meaningful after all!
Heart: I thought so.

—⁂—

When I was seven my heart was broken when a spoilsport kid from the neighborhood told me Santa Claus wasn't real. Observational science was not in my corner on this one. I was crushed, for I needed something bigger than this world to exist, something outside to make a grand entrance and rescue me; and in my heart, Santa qualified. I went home and asked my mother to correct the kid's impertinence, though perhaps not in those words. She settled me down, then got down to eye level and tenderly explained, "No, Santa's not real, but hope is, and so is the love that's in here." Then she put her hand over my heart. It was a beautiful gift and I've never forgotten it. Afterward, I was satisfied, mostly, and headed back outside to play, wondering if I'd still be getting Christmas presents.

Some fifty years later I still carry what I learned that day in my heart: the scoffers don't get the last word, the lovers do.

Chapter 8

EXPOSED

The ground is level at the foot of the cross

BILLY GRAHAM

The Lion roared, and I awoke to a different world than the one I thought I was in for my first thirty-six years. I found out that Santa's not real, but that love is, and it comes from God. That the material world is not all there is—there is a scene behind the scene where the real story unfolds. That gods will let me down, but that God never will. That I am no longer on a path to nowhere fast, but smack in the middle of an eternal journey into God's heart. That the love of the body of Christ got me over the line. And most pressing of all, I learned that my wife and children needed to be on my same side of that line at all costs.

I remember when Jesus was closing in on me, how one day I stood in the kitchen with my wife Karen (not Siever), sharing where

I was in my search, and being overcome with a feeling of uncleanliness, guilt, and outright exposure. I told her I felt like we were Adam and Eve right after the fall. It was an extraordinary experience topped only by the fact that she said she felt it too. Three months later we both knew Jesus as Savior. It took me a lifetime of seeking, straining, and striving in a quest to find the meaning of life—to find God. Apparently some hearts are more ready than others. Praise God. My wife saw what I was seeing, and the heart of a Lover won hers.

By that time we had moved an hour outside of Atlanta to get away from the bustle and to raise our four children on a farm. Not the chicken and cow kind. The kind with a barn jam-packed with household overflow, a pasture that doubled as an oversized yard often visited by flocks of seed-pecking blackbirds and graced by big arcing moons you could touch. In the middle sat a blue-gray ranch-style home where I rocked on a wide porch under a slow paddle fan. Not the Ponderosa, but I wasn't complaining. It was a wonderful place to enjoy a quieter life, observe nature, take leisurely strolls with the dogs, and talk with God. I came to Jesus in that house. All six of us did.

Once my wife and I were together in our faith, we knew we needed to get ourselves and the kids to church right away. We found a classic quaint church in the country with a tall white beacon of a steeple, surrounded by flowering myrtles and filled with welcoming people. It was a mainline denomination with a subdued worship style—a subject I didn't have an opinion about yet. I simply followed what I heard: Get thee to a church.

We listened to pleasant sermons, sang old hymns, made quick friends, and my spirit soared. But there was an unsettled part of me that felt like I was learning a new language, and I was concerned about getting it right. Before long this is what I learned about my new language: Now that I was a Christian, the way to be a better one was go to church every Sunday, attend Sunday school class, read the Bible every day, tithe regularly, and pray daily, for starters. I was excited about doing all of that at first, but soon began to wonder why the list to become a Christian was so much shorter. 1) Accept a free gift by faith. 2) Finally rest. Though they were fine people, and their faith was genuine, I felt pressure to conform, and since I'm not good at that, I became restless. Something was amiss.

Nevertheless, I took to Sunday school class like a retriever to a tennis ball. I was starting to learn my way around the Bible now—baby steps they're called—and began to speak up more confidently, and sometimes overconfidently. One regrettable time I was in the middle of making what I was sure would be a crowd-pleasing point when I referenced the book of "Philippinese" for scholarly emphasis. The correction from the teacher was gentle but swift, and as I couldn't persuade the class that there was in fact a sixty-seventh book of the Bible, I decided to accept my humble pie while making a mental note for next week's class not to pronounce Galatians with a hard "t."

Embarrassments aside, the Bible study was enriching, though I did continue to feel like something wasn't quite right. A few months later I decided to take my concerns to the pastor, a mild-mannered scholarly type from Somewhere, Tennessee.

"Where do I go from here, Pastor? I've accepted Christ. Now what?"

He looked at me like he'd never heard such a thing. Then along with a disinterested shrug he gave me this stellar advice: "I guess ya just go deeper."

I guess? "How do I do that?" I asked in my hopeful best.

The pastor, looking down at his shoes, then clarified the whole of life. "Ya just do."

"Ah, wonderful," I lied, now looking down at my shoes. "Good, good," I added, all the while thinking my sarcastic worst. "That's it! I'll just go deeper. Thanks for the big tip. See you around the ol' altar, Pastor!"

I came to him spiritually lean and hungry, and left inwardly steaming. To me, back then, he was the pastor. I was the flock. And that meant he was line and I was staff, in quite the spiritually immature state at that. I didn't expect him to have all the answers, but a little guidance, please.

The journey into God's heart was not going to be tidy.

I later got an inkling of why his answer was so mutteringly thin when, while I was in Sunday school class asking questions, debating, and parsing the finer points of some doctrine—in other words being myself—the pastor's wife wasn't having any of it and interjected from across the room, "Come on! Let's face it, the Bible is full of mistakes."

I looked around and noticed all other heads were down (looking at their shoes maybe). Not one person reacted—not outwardly at least—and my heart sank. I joined the class as a new Christian with a clear conviction of certain unbending truths. Biblical inerrancy was one of them. I never believed her statement for a second. Years of seeking, studying apologetics, and meeting with intelligent men of faith had prepared me for this moment, and I'm proud to report I replied in my tactful best, "That's total hogwash!" or some such. After the ensuing brusque and thorough "exchange of ideas," neither of us changed the other's mind, and no one else spoke up.

Between these two disconcerting first church experiences and the fact that the entire denomination was caught up in the wash of a church-split over an encroaching liberal doctrine that I wasn't buying either, it was time to move on. Not long after we left that church, I heard the pastor and his wife had relocated to another church across town, to dispense their brand of Christian uncertainty perhaps. Either way, hopefully they grabbed on to the deepest part of the faith, God Himself, and grew in their journeys. Though, admittedly, that wasn't how I was thinking at the time.

We moved on to a larger church with my faith undeterred, and my hunger to go deeper into God's heart, and therefore my own, growing. The kids loved the more active and larger environment, and faster than angels fly we found ourselves happily immersed in a new church life where the pastor spoke a bit of fire and brimstone, old Southern style, and I stayed rooted in the Bible, rooted like a wild tree.

Chapter 9

TO MY BELOVED CHILD

Man has counted:
The Bible contains 66 books,
1,189 chapters, 31,103 verses,
and one heart behind them all.

AUTHOR'S CONVICTION

I was recently asked to name my favorite books of all time. I didn't hesitate to respond. The Bible and Dick and Jane were one and two. As the words sprang forth, I was astounded at the distance I had come. Step by step it's not so noticeable, but when you look back the whole winding way, you realize that you're a different person. The journey of a thousand miles begins with a single step, so the expression goes.[16] In a way mine began with a single page. I refer to the day when the tenant next door asked me about the Bible and I declared it a "good book," never having read it; how

I went home, opened to Genesis, and read the first page. It wasn't what I expected and I couldn't stop.

The Bible is not God, not the fourth person of the Trinity, nor, contrary to the impression given by some sermons I've heard, the third Person of the Trinity—Father, Son, and Holy Bible. We are not to "live by the Bible," nor its Ten Commandments. We can't. The Jews of the Old Testament found that out the hard way. Nor does the Bible contain *every* word of God. He talks to us in other ways, does He not? I like how Dallas Willard explains it. "While the Bible is the written Word of God, the word of God is not simply the Bible."[17]

The Bible is history, prophecy, instruction, and so much more. Foremost, the Bible is a love letter from the Lover to His beloved. It is a personal and relational invitation to intimacy. It is not a book of rules and regulations to beat each other over the head with. Had I known that earlier, I could have avoided a lot of grief. For years, I used the Bible as a debating tool. Or I tackled it like my college textbooks, breaking down the parts and often missing the whole. Or I turned it into a head exercise that I could master, which can't be done by mere mortals in any case. A love letter is read with the heart and grows in meaning as the reader grows more in love. Indeed it takes the mind to understand it, but it's the heart that feels it.

Early on I was drawn to Ecclesiastes because it spoke to the anguish I had carried in my soul for so long. However, the book that spoke the loudest was Romans. I loved the way it blended both logic and lyricism to present the fullness of the gospel. Given my propensity for miring in the analytical, though, I often rushed through its lyrical parts and became overly academic with my approach. That is a recipe for a stilted faith.

To balance my growth I would try moving into a book like Psalms, aware that many have hailed it as the most accessible to the heart. But as one who practiced for a lifetime to hold my feelings down, I found it hard to connect with. For that reason, Psalms was at first surprisingly inaccessible to me. Clearly I hadn't fully grasped that its words—all the words of the Bible—have supernatural power.

I well knew the immense value of plumbing the depths of the Bible with the mind, of seeking to memorize and understand its words. The Bible is true north, after all, and it orients its readers to truth in the same way that studying a dollar bill heightens awareness of the counterfeits. Yes, I knew the depths of truth went on and on, but I didn't realize then that the heart dimensions of the Bible are inexhaustible too. It only took me two decades to learn that beautiful fact.

You'll not be shocked to hear that I still love to study my Bible these days. What's new is that I have also learned to enjoy the times when I meditate over its words without having to do anything analytical with them. It is a matter of truth that "the word of God is alive and active" (Hebrews 4:12), and thus, come to find out, those words don't need me to tackle them to harness their power. My role is to let them soak into my soul and trust an all-knowing God to use them how and when He pleases. I've discovered that those are the times I hear God most clearly and grow closer to His heart anyway. And that is the goal, is it not?

The power of God's Word came to life for me one miraculous afternoon during a visit with my paternal grandfather—he who taught me to enjoy the beauties of a well-cultivated yard; who sat me on his lap and scratched across my face with his unshaved whiskers while holding me tightly with affection; who never met a pun he didn't like; who taught me how to sit back and savor a Sunday afternoon golf match on TV; whose hobby was adoring my grandmother; and who well into his 70s, if I dropped by unannounced in the early evening, would answer the door in a disheveled robe because he and my grandmother were still amorous, God bless them. Too much information? Perhaps, perhaps not; but it is a relevant fact. He was an all-around great guy and the gentlest of souls.

And now he was ninety. He mostly sat in his chair those days and watched television. He was never the same after Grandmother died, other than that he had the same sweet soul. As I visited with him, I nervously awaited my chance to read the verses on the card I held in my hand, the ones out of the Book of Romans I was told were a six-verse step-by-step pathway to lead someone to Christ. They call it the "Roman Road" and it's been an effective evangelism tool for ages, though I'd never considered using it. I guess till then I thought I had better words that would add some needed razzmatazz into the explaining. Nevertheless, I resigned myself to trying it as a noble experiment. This is how it went.

"Hey Granddad, what do you think about God?"

"Oh, I don't know." He smiled at me, then looked back at the TV. He and I had never talked about anything close to this.

I sneaked a look at my first verse. "Did you know that all of us 'have sinned, and fall short of the glory of God'?" (Romans 3:23). He was paying more attention to me now, making it harder for me to retrieve the next verse. A minute passed. "The wages of sin is death," I continued. "But the free gift of God is eternal life in Christ Jesus our Lord" (6:23). Another minute, then more boldly: "Granddad, the Bible says that 'God demonstrates His own love toward us, in that while we were yet sinners, Christ died for us'" (5:8). And on it went, till a couple of verses later I got to the part, "If you confess with your mouth Jesus as Lord, and believe in your heart that God raised Him from the dead, you will be saved" (10:9).

At which point he looked straight at me and said, "I want to do that."

"Really?" I don't know what I expected, but it wasn't that.

"Yeah, I want to accept Jesus."

All told, it took less than ten minutes for him to come to that decision. Or ninety years and six verses depending on how you look at it. After I got over my that-was-entirely-too-easy hesitation, we prayed together and he received Jesus as his Savior that day.

My granddad died in his sleep two years later and entered Paradise. My reunion with him is going to be sweet.

There's dynamite in those words.

—⚹—

There's an enduring image of a young lady who pulls off the petals of a flower one by one, proclaiming, "He loves me, he loves me not, he loves me, he loves me not," as she hopes the last petal confirms he does, in fact love her. When I pick up a Bible, I'm reminded that for us, the bride of Christ, we get to release each petal to the heavens and shout, "He loves me! He loves me! He loves me! He loves me!…"

I felt that love even before I knew God, way back in my Dick and Jane days, and I feel it through the words of the Bible now. And with that pleasing thought, I'd like to broaden my earlier answer. My two favorite books are more than just books to me. They are bookends, and my journey of faith will always be swaddled between them.

Chapter 10

Hanging Out with Dad

It was my first Pinewood Derby as a dad, as an anything. I wasn't a "wind tunnel" dad; I was the other kind, who after several failed attempts in my makeshift workshop said, "You'll do fine, son." And he did. I put on the wheels, he did the decorating, and a block of white wood with lightning pinstripes and wobbly wheels came in third place in the Cub Scout Pinewood Derby. I was proud.

The next year I decided to get more involved so that my son could compete with all those other dads (I mean Cub Scouts) who used their dads' Lockheed-Martin connections to make aerodynamic masterpieces that traveled Mach 1. If you don't count the piece of car sliding ahead of our competitor at the finish, we came in dead last. I had no mechanical pride to begin with, so I took it well. Our car was a straggly mess, but that didn't matter. The best part of the day was spending time with my son, just hanging out.

We did a lot of that in those days with our new church family. They were the most friendly, Deep South, how's-yer-mom'n'em, down-to-earth people I'd ever had the pleasure of fellowshipping with. It was full-scale wholesome, complete with church picnics, smiling choirs, and passionate sermons; and they said "fixin'" a lot. But I also saw another side working in the church that troubled me. I was being taught a conditional, performance-based relationship with God that overshadowed the unconditional one that had captured my heart from the beginning.

We were in the middle of our pleasing whirl of activities and good times when, after one particular sermon, and then another and another and another, I began to notice a pattern (it takes me four). I kept hearing accusations that made me think I wasn't doing enough, getting involved enough, and mostly being good enough. At some point in most of these sermons I was told I was a sinner who needed to clean up my act for God before I could enjoy His fellowship again. I needed fixin'. It was true I was no choir boy, though in my defense, I had some friends in the choir and they weren't either!

As I say, I had no illusions. I knew I was flawed. But as I understood the gospel, I never started out as a good person deserving to be forgiven anyway. I was the problem through and through. That's why I gave my life to Jesus. Apparently now, so I was being told, I needed to clean up my mess, to be "good" before I could hang out with God. And for a while I bought the lie. It wasn't hard, truth be told. At some level I wanted to earn my keep to prove to God I was worthy to be at His table.

So I got to work trying to live up to my church-imposed, self-imposed benchmarks of good behavior, and summarily, predictably failed. I kept trying to hold it all together, but the pieces kept coming off. And within a couple of years, I had gone from having faith as wide-eyed and unguarded as a child on his daddy's lap, to being all stiff and nervous around God, performing to gain a father's approval, not to mention that of my pewmates. Spending time around the table with family is supposed to be relaxing and festive. This was work. Moreover, as I was to learn, this whole idea of earning my keep, of bringing my own goodness to the table, is the alienating thorn in the souls of all men, and its name is pride (see Adam and Eve for reference), and it is everywhere.

Once, in the early days of my faith, I found myself engaged in a heart-to-heart conversation about God with a dear relative, and I asked if she thought she would go to Heaven when she died.

"Yes, I'm a good person," was the reply.

Then I changed my approach and asked if she had ever received Jesus as her Savior.

Again, "You know, I'm a good person so I believe I'm going to Heaven."

Next I threw in my personal favorite. "Does it make sense that God is grading us on a sliding scale of good deeds? If that were the case, what if Mother Teresa were the minimum standard? We'd be in big trouble. On the other hand, if it's Hitler, we're in!" I pressed on. "Where do you fit on that scale?"

I had high hopes it was all sinking in and was even thinking how well the conversation was going when she interrupted my mirth to repeat herself. "Yeah, well, I am a good person. I've always done good things."

Thud.

And round and round we went. A self-proclaimed good person is the hardest kind to reach. A self-*made* good person comes in a close second.

Not long after that "meaning of life" conversation, I was engaged in another, this time with a longtime friend. We spent several hours talking and I shared with him about my journey and how I learned the truth that God is Who the Bible says He is after all. To my delight he agreed with all of it, the entire gospel, even acknowledging, "I know I'm not good enough and that I need Jesus…"

I was about to jump in full bore with an "Okay so then…" and lead him through to the big finish when he continued.

"But I'm not ready to accept Jesus yet. There are some things I need to clean up first."

Oh brother. I tried to back up and explain to him he had the order wrong, but he held his ground. "I want to work it out on my terms," he said.

As far as I know he's still working on it.

When I became a follower of Jesus, I was well aware of the deal—there was nothing I could do to earn my way into God's good graces. Jesus already did that for me and then He welcomed me to a relationship, broken as I was. But now barely a new follower of Jesus, I was beginning to think that it somehow depended on my efforts to stay in the relationship. And that didn't feel right.

Thankfully I didn't wallow in that frame of mind for long as a few good men pointed me in the right direction and I was able to recognize the error of my thinking; though regrettably, still today the behavior emerges, here and there. It will be a lifelong grapple.

It is one of the bankrupt proclivities of mankind—to kid ourselves into thinking we can clean ourselves up and fix our own behavior. No wonder I tend to avoid God when I'm in a bad state, running off until I'm "cleaned up" enough to be back in His presence. How that must sadden my Heavenly Father, when because I have some latest problem or issue, I run from the only One Who can fix it, not to mention comfort me in the process. Philippians 1:6 promises that "He who began a good work in you will carry it on to completion until the day of Christ Jesus" (NIV). Too often I forget that, and I miss hanging out with Dad when I do.

We all knew that our new church had an unwritten code of behavior that we must conform to, the implication being that if we didn't, although our salvation was secure, we risked losing God's fellowship and favor, so we were taught. Lying, cheating, and stealing were all on the list; certainly adultery made it (both the heart-kind and the corporeal kind); not attending church was on it; pride and envy—permanent fixtures; on the other hand, gossip rarely made it, nor did meddling; and gluttony, particularly at the church picnic, was never, ever on it. Blessed relief! At least I didn't have to feel guilty about that extra slice, two if I'm not lying.

Every Sunday in church, at the end of the service there would be a call for any who felt led to come forward to either accept Jesus as Savior or to kneel at the altar to confess some sin (other than gluttony I would think). If no one came forward, the call ratcheted upwards.

"Is anyone out there feelin' the need?" Silence. "Perhaps toward the back?" Not even a faint rustling. "Do I hear someone in pew four, pew five? Somebody? Anybody!" Not a creature was stirring. Till finally, "Ray Jackson, would you come up here already!"

I kid about Ray, of course, but it could get downright desperate. One day it was, "No one leaves till someone comes forward!" A few minutes later some hungry soul finally did, but whether the hunger was for food or Jesus, that I don't know.

At such times it felt more like orchestrating an outcome rather than letting God unfold one. Mercifully there were always certain people who would finally go forward while others just looked at their watches. I was a watch-looker.

All in all, they were good people who liked to call themselves "sinners," who in between their self-effort moments were being made better by God. They certainly understood the priority of Jesus, as did I. What I didn't understand was why all the yelling. I didn't take to it then and still don't. I know it's part and parcel of fire and brimstone preaching, but I've never responded to this idea of scaring you out of Hell (there's a cursing way of putting that but it got washed out with soap). For me, I knew of my depravity, but needing the love of God and desiring to spend time with Him were the motivations. I was running toward God, not running from Satan, being as I was drawn to the relationship, as all of His children are. I'm sure it's really two sides of the same coin. Hell is another word for lonely without end and if God's not there, we don't want any part of it.

Different people respond to different approaches, I suppose, and I have to remember that God draws us as He wills. We're the ones who get to say yes or no.

———

For a summer of Saturdays I helped my dad build a fence around his farmland south of Atlanta. We plunged into the task; battled humid forests, steep-banked creeks, and ill-tempered briars; and sometimes we even built the fence.

Still and all it was a good summer to hang out with Dad. We built to the backdrop of my trying to convince him that the God of the Bible was real. Dig. Argue. Hammer. Bleed. Repeat. That was my fence-building technique as well as my evangelism one. And though I felt like I was doing all the bleeding, in retrospect I'm sure we both were. I had little chance of convincing an intelligent, highly-trained attorney of anything, let alone that God was, well, God. As a young boy I had to offer a cogent defense for why I shouldn't have to finish my green beans before having dessert, and to my recollection, for the duration of childhood I ate every insidious bean that ever crossed my plate. The mission ahead would be daunting.

Mangled fingers improved my hammering and mangled pride softened my heart enough to deliver the message, and toward summer's end I became adequate at both. I made marked progress in our Saturday talks the day I figured out that my best approach was to take "me" out of the equation and simply give him books to read that addressed his particular objections, one at a time, week after week. These happened to be, providentially, the same apologetic books that appealed to me during my own search.

"Is there truly such a thing as morality?"

"Ah, got just the book for you, Dad. C.S. Lewis's *Mere Christianity*."

"Okay I get that there's a God, but how do we know there's not more than one?"

Righto. Here's your light reading for the week: *Summa Theologica* by Thomas Aquinas.

And he'd be right back the next week. "How do we know we're not God?"

I resisted asking, "If that's the case then why is God trudging through these boggy creeks building a fence?" and instead handed him the next book.

On it went, from the resurrection appearances to the eyewitness accounts, from man's sin to the historical reliability of the Bible. And to my dad's credit, and really to God's, he read every book with an open mind. Whenever he was satisfied a particular objection was overcome, he'd move right on to the next book, till ultimately he found himself at the brink of a ledge with nothing left to do but jump, which I'm happy to say he did.

Some have commented as a means of encouragement that I'm the reason my dad came to Christ. I appreciate the sentiment, always, but don't believe it, and that's not manufactured humility. What I did was hang out with my dad that summer. I was clumsy, uptight, half-baked for the task, and only knew to try to keep up with him, feeling a lot like I was holding the tail of a tiger the whole way. That was the tangible, but what really happened was Jesus drew my dad into His heart and proposed, not with codes of conduct, but with an offer of eternal love, to which my dad, at the sprightly age of sixty, said, "Yes, I do."

Today, nearly twenty years later, he teaches Sunday school for the senior citizens at his church, and he is a gifted apologist with mangled fingers.

A month or so after Dad accepted Christ, he asked me, "How do I know I really meant it when I asked Jesus into my life?"

A ready illustration came to mind. "Did you know what you were doing when a few moments ago you flipped on the light switch in the hallway?"

"Say that again?" I admit it was a bit from left field.

"Did you want that light on and know that if you flipped the switch it would in fact turn on?"

There was no hesitation. "Yes, of course I did."

"And did you mean it?"

He just smiled.

And right away my mind drifted back to our days in Miami when he used to charge me a dime for leaving the light on. Money well spent, I thought.

Chapter 11

THIS WALK OF FAITH

*Faith is the highest passion in a
man...no one gets further.*

SØREN KIERKEGAARD

If a tree falls in the forest and no one is there to hear it does it
make a sound? That's a dimwitted question to pose, even for a
philosopher. Of course it does; surely God hears it. The Bible is
clear on the matter: "He is before all things, and in Him all things
hold together" (Colossians 1:17). In fact, if God didn't exist there
would be no trees anyway, or forests, or oceans or skies, or you or
me; only nothingness, which isn't possible, but that's a different
affair.

If I'm alone and I fall in the forest will anyone hear? That's
what my seeking heart always hungered to know. I'd like to answer
that here and now: Count on it! The omniscient, omnibenevolent,

omnipresent Alpha and Omega, Who has numbered all the remaining hairs on my head, will hear! And when I reflect on that reality and, moreover, on the staggering reality that He chose to make me at all, my heart sings out: "I am fearfully and wonderfully made" (Psalm 139:14). He, on the other hand, has always existed, and therefore, His words majestically subsume mine. "I Am," He proclaims.

Before I knew God, I had already reasoned that if this life is all there is, it amounts to a life of nothing. Once I found Him, by increasing measures, a different conclusion became undeniably true: He is sovereign, the heartbeat and meaning in everything that is good in my life—family, friends, health, home, work, play, hopes, dreams, and perhaps most revealing of all, my faith.

I see a man I admire. Here he comes, on fire for the Lord, his life a living testimony, so humble, so trusting of God, so comfortably certain, so all in. He exudes faith. He's a good man. But I catch myself envying him, and worse, idolizing him—a mere man—and in the process overlooking that his faith, same as mine, is dependent upon the God Who sparks it. What am I thinking!? My faith is not in faith, is it? That is thinner than air. No, my faith is palpable and it is placed in God. It is my bona fide connection to God's Spirit within, and without it I can do nothing lasting or good. And for those reasons, when it reflects God's glory, that's to His credit, not mine or any man's.

Faith is the road that led me to Jesus, and I have been slow to see that, astonishingly, God intends to lead me deeper into His heart by that same faith. For too long I have distorted the truth and tried to act my way into God's heart. But faith works from the other direction.

When faith is resolute and well-placed, it is God Who pulls me in, and it is God Who inspires the thoughts which lead to right actions and God-ordained outcomes. This is why, with enough faith, we can stand up to the greatest oppression. With enough faith, we have courage to enter the lion's den (though in my case, I'm hoping God precludes the possibility after considering my low pain threshold). With enough faith, we accomplish the most good, we experience overwhelming joy even in the face of the greatest challenges, and we do it all with a power we access, but cannot manufacture or summon. We can only enter it with a ready heart. God is sovereign over the fullness of life's journey and we only ever receive anything lasting and good by relying on Him in faith.

This fact of God's sovereignty leads me to an astounding truth: Not even my doubt is mine alone. If He is the God of my faith, He is also the God of my doubt. My doubt arises when I give in to the enemy's temptations, or when I demand to know what I can't see, or when I pout and hide because God won't orchestrate my preferred outcome. Yet the unfaithful person never experiences doubts like these, for he never believes in God to begin with (read that again—several times if need be). But I choose—that's the word- "choose"—by faith to place my trust in the God of everything, knowing that His love is so persevering that He'll love me not only when I'm standing in the light; He'll love me even when I'm stumbling through the dark.

Just as I should know better than to extol a man for his faith, the same holds true for any righteous behavior of my fellow man. His good behavior can't come out of his innate character—it has a better chance of springing from the ether. Rather, it is instilled by God through that faith.

Consider closely the virtue of bravery. It can never be, "My! Oh my! Would you look at Brother Larry battling on the front lines for God. How brave he is! Isn't he terrific? I wish I were brave like him." For it is actually, "Look at Larry, a man after God's own heart, a man of deep faith and used often by God." Without God animating Larry, through Larry's faith, brave Larry is as cowardly as the rest of us. It is God in Larry, not Larry for God. And if Larry is doing these acts on his own apart from God, it's called selfishness anyway, or foolhardiness. Certainly not bravery. And I'm sorry to bring you into all this, Larry, but you well know where we must put our faith. Acting brave is an act. To be brave takes faith, which you, Larry, have in abundance.

When I reflect on any virtue I've ever demonstrated, from love to kindness, from humility to perseverance (me, me, me, me), there is no getting away from it—my pride be darned—God gets the credit for them all, for they only ever appear in the context of my faith in Him. If not, what am I worshiping here? Me, Myself, and I? Heaven help me. I might as well try to take credit for my own salvation.

The Bible makes clear that helping old ladies cross the road (which I acknowledge I've never done, though I did help an old man cross the town square once) is nice to do, but it won't get anyone into Heaven. Only faith in Jesus will do that. And lest I ever get too big for my britches, I do well to recognize the same truth applies to reaching others for Christ.

Yes, I'm enjoined to "always be prepared to give an answer to everyone who asks you to give the reason for the hope that you have" (1 Peter 3:15, NIV). But suppose I'm in an obstinate mood on the day some seeker crosses my path, the day he asks me, "Who is this Jesus fella anyway?" And though sensing God wants me to stay and talk, I respond, "Sorry bud. I'm too busy to chit-chat today," and then walk away with a tough-luck-friend shrug. Did he just miss his big chance? He "coulda been somebody" and now, because of me, he has a one-way ticket to H-E-double hockey sticks?[18] Not at all. For I can't be his answer. Only Jesus can.

My disobedience to God's promptings will never excuse anyone. God knows ahead of time when I'll shrink back and fail, and it is in His just character to give every ready soul enough time and the right conditions in this life to put their faith in Jesus alone. There is no excuse. Even so, man is prone to rationalizing, though of course when I do it I have a good reason.

I try to find the humor, but it is a sad fact that without faith, even miracles get rationalized away. How many miracles can you count when you walk through the forest? Some see none. Just nature being nature they say. I say: see that tree? Miracle! The breeze? Miracle! The birds? Together now, miracles! How else would you explain how they got here? Take your time with your answer, friend, we've got all eternity.

Whether occurring over epochal spans or in a moment in time, miracles are everywhere. In all cases they are made and superintended by an almighty God. In his book *God in the Dock*, C.S. Lewis illustrates this brilliantly when he writes that when Jesus turned water into wine in Cana, it was no more a miracle than the natural processes of the world: "God creates the vine and teaches it to draw up water by its roots and, with the aid of the sun, to turn that water into a juice which will ferment and take on certain qualities. Thus every year, from Noah's time till ours, God turns water into wine."[19]

If the principle applies to a vine, how much more to the daily rhythms of our bodies, held together by Him; and to our souls which, year after year, depend on His Spirit within to live out this journey of faith. These are miracles, are they not? Then again, all matters of faith are. Those few flickering moments when I see that clearly, it is an almost incomprehensible joy. If God is sovereign over all of my journey, then the pressure to generate a performance is off. I can simply place all my faith in Him to lead me through.

A blessed assurance to be sure, yet mostly I succumb to the temptation to hold some of it back in an effort to manage how life should go. Foolish me! If I can't cut the mustard by my own efforts in regard to salvation, then a fury of self-effort to be a good Christian won't work for my sanctification either—and here I promised I wouldn't use fancy jargon. Let me try again: then it won't work for my journey into the heart of God either. "Are you so foolish? After beginning by means of the Spirit, are you now trying to finish by means of the flesh?" (Galatians 3:3, NIV) That's a rhetorical question, brother Paul. I already said I was.

Even so, Lord knows, I pray daily that He'll cut this foolishness out of me until all my faith resides in Him.

I realize my heart already knows much of this—it is the seat of my faith after all—but my flesh forgets, spends too much time in the pull of the world. Still, I do feel God working in me, particularly those days I find the time to walk through the woods behind my home, a place that gives me space from the world's commotion, that unmasks my pride, a place where my faith grows stronger.

Usually I walk the familiar path by the sycamores that bend to reach the sky; I cross the creek, hoping to see the shadows of the hawks, which always make me smile; then work my way along the bank near where the beetles crawl, and clamber over the big tree that fell, I know not when, but certainly with a thud. I walk faithfully along my merry way, fully aware that God sees all these miracles too. This I know for certain, because I never walk alone.

All the earth is here because of the grace of God, and by the grace of God so am I.

Chapter 12

Relentless Grace

Reach out and experience the breadth! Test its
length! Plumb the depths! Rise to the heights!
Live full lives, full in the fullness of God.

Ephesians 3:18 (The Message)

Several years after joining our church, I enthusiastically accepted the responsibility and challenge of teaching Sunday school. In between misplacing my prepared lessons and my habit of toppling easels, I actually taught quite mediocrely. Read on, you'll agree.

I got some parts right. We had good fellowship and I knew how to learn, but I didn't know how to teach, which was somewhat of a requirement for the post. So I winged it, my overall thrust being to teach the reasons why the church needed to be a relational-based and not a performance-based family. Funny, it didn't occur to me to practice that in class. As is my lifetime habit, I made it into a head thing instead and turned what I believe was rather good source material (the Bible) into the Mojave Desert. My soul was missing the one thing needed to teach Sunday school the right way: water. I noticed I wasn't alone.

One day after a particularly parched sermon, I went up to the pastor and, in my most diplomatic manner, said something like, "Wonderful sermon, Pastor. By the way, do you have any plans to ever (translation: in my lifetime would be nice) do a sermon on the grace of God? I've been studying it recently and there might just be something in it. Anyway, I'd sure love to learn more about that so I can go deeper in my faith."

Then, all pleasant as Southern tea, he spoke these unforgettable words: "Ya know, you can go too far with that grace stuff. Givin' people a free license to sin is askin' for trouble."

I had been studying and had a zinger of a retort. "Seems like we were sinning pretty good under the law already." Unfortunately, though, those were not the words I spoke. They only sprang to mind as I was driving home.

I tuned back in to his concluding remarks. "When people sin under grace they're only turnin' what God did into cheap grace, anyway."

Now I was ready, with my actual words, spoken regrettably in an indelicate tone. "Cheap? God paid the ultimate price of sacrificing His Son on the cross. Exactly how much do you want grace to cost?"

His set jaw and quavering temples told me we were done. I managed a tight smile, mumbled something along the lines of,

"Kind of thought the truth was supposed to set us free," then averted my eyes and backed away by measures, kind of like you would from a bear who is considering you for dinner.

I felt bad for putting the pastor on the spot, but worse about the attempt made to shackle my soul, and I wasn't going to let the matter rest. So being more eager student than wise congregant, I committed to spend an indeterminate time (turns out it will be eternity) to study on my own this vital, now-preoccupying subject of grace. This is the essence of what I've learned so far:

The Christian journey is one of unconditional freedom. Although we can misuse our freedom to indulge the flesh, without question we are free and will remain so. Every follower of Jesus shares in the declaration, "Christ lives in me" (Galatians 2:20). For that reason there will never be a need for a wall around us again. We are sheep in an open pasture, and we live in the fullness and deliverance of grace, not under one smidgen of law. That's a good thing.

However, the law still exists to condemn anyone who rejects Jesus as Savior, and it is more than able to trip up any child of God who forgets he is free and tries to live by its mandates. That's a revealing thing.

For it means, contrary to what seems to tickle our pride, grace doesn't lead one to sin; the law does that! I have that on good authority: "Nevertheless, I would not have known what sin was had it not been for the law. For I would not have known what coveting really was if the law had not said, "You shall not covet" (Romans

7:7, NIV). So unless I'm missing something, the sure way to stir up sin is to be under the law, which God's children will never be again, for we are "not under law, but under grace" (Romans 6:14). Jesus made sure of that when He died on the cross. And that's a "Hallelujah!" thing if ever there was one.

So then, how can I, as the pastor stated, "go too far with grace" (shrug, muse, shrug some more)? The question perplexes because it's a first-rate category error. There is nothing I can do with grace but receive it, for grace is what Jesus does. It is His unending gift of love. Can we go too far with love? How about kindness? Forgiveness?

We know the rub. The pride of the flesh wants to contribute to the deal, while in our hearts we know we can't. What does the God of the universe need from us? He privileges us to be a part of the journey, to receive all He has to offer, and it's a viscous, wearying cycle when we try to do what only God can. Such is the treadmill of a performance-based religion that comes from the perspective of needing to behave like a good person to stay in good standing with my Father and to earn His approval.

Jesus didn't take kindly to the Pharisees of His day who commandeered the law and added a bevy of new laws to "justify" themselves before God, all done largely to impress others to boot. And it is an affront to Jesus now, whenever we act as if what He did wasn't enough. Man's problem isn't cheap grace. It's cheap works!

The short version: our ever-loving Savior offers an invitation into an unconditional relationship, one where I have been freed from the law and where my good standing is assured for all eternity.

It's easy to miss.

The woman at the well failed to grasp the invitation to an eternal relationship that was being extended to her, though she was staring right into the face of the Savior of the world.

"Jesus answered her, 'If you knew the gift of God and who it is that asks you for a drink, you would have asked him and He would have given you living water.' 'Sir,' the woman said, 'you have nothing to draw with and the well is deep. Where can you get this living water?'...

Jesus answered, 'Everyone who drinks of this water will be thirsty again, but whoever drinks the water I give them will never thirst. Indeed, the water I give them will become in them a spring of water welling up to eternal life'" (John 4:10-11, 13,14, NIV).

I didn't miss my invitation, praise God. In a single moment, I received the gift of eternal life. What I miss all too often, however, is that by the grace of God, the Water of Life continually wells up within my spirit to guide my steps while I'm still here in this temporal state. I don't have to perform to gain my Father's approval. All I have to do is drink. Which to be fair with myself, often I do. That is, when I'm not circling the well for stubbornly long stretches, acting like I'm under the law, and wondering why my soul feels so dry.

Lord, teach me to soak my soul in the Water of Life and never stop!

"Fair enough," say certain killjoys, "a life of grace is one that is relational and free-flowing. All well and true. But don't forget there are consequences for our bad behavior when we stray." Agreed.

But why, I always wonder, are they so quick to go there? When someone is admiring the beauty of a flower on the bank of a brook, what gloomy sourpuss chooses that time to say, "Yeah, but look at those weeds on the far bank"? We're talking about grace and all that flows from it—joy and freedom and hope and the goodness of life, and eternity with our loving Father. Stand back, killjoys! Yes there are consequences when we stray. Loving fathers always seek to teach their children, but not with condemnation. That may be what you're dishing out, but Romans 8:1 won't have it: "Therefore there is now no condemnation for those who are in Christ Jesus."

Our Father is a lover, not an authoritarian punisher. It is the law that condemns souls and sends them into hiding, and God's grace that changes them through love. And without question, He desires to transform each of our souls by irresistibly lavishing us with that love until we are lovers too, with big, graceful hearts.

I thank God that even when I don't practice what I preach, His relentless grace will continue to pour. That's the real short version.

Chapter 13

THE ARTIST

I enjoy painting these days. It is a new-found pleasure and I'm not that good at it. Most times what I imagine in my mind and what ends up daubed across the canvas are, to be charitable, remarkably unalike. For that reason I have learned to stay away from the direct representation of what I'm conjuring and to focus instead on a more impressionistic approach. It's harder for others to discern if I met my goal. But I know. I can always feel it when it's done.

It used to bother me, not being able to sort it all out. But I've come to accept that when I pick up the artist's brush, the final result will always be a mystery. I believe that's why I enjoy it so much.

—⁓—

There are certain mysteries I'll never sort out. I can't begin to explain how you create something out of nothing, or speak a world into existence, or make a man from dust and give him free will and the capacity to love, or how to set my alarm clock in the hotel room. I won't even try. I have a more foolhardy ambition in mind—I'm going to try to explain the Trinity.

The Trinity will always be a beautiful mystery, thank God. And I do thank Him often. Sometimes I thank Him as Father, other times as Jesus, but as the Holy Spirit, curiously never, although I suppose I could. And if you ever hear me saying, "Thank You, Three Person Godhead," you'll know I'm putting on airs.

Since the day I first stepped into a church, I have heard many sermons on God the Father and God the Son, even a few on the concept of the Trinity, but next to none about God the Holy Spirit. Once during a sermon I heard this glancing definition: He's just the love between the Father and the Son. *Just* the love? What is God, a binity? Surely, the third person of the Trinity—i.e. God!—deserved more air time than what I was hearing early on.

It has improved over time, maybe because my ears got tuned—thank You, Three Person Godhead. However, even today, the Holy Spirit gets scant mention in most sermons I hear, which makes no sense. Leaving the Holy Spirit out of the equation is like trying to inspire an artist by handing him a tube of paint instead of showing him the sunrise.

The Scriptures say, "Do you not know that you are a temple of God and that the Spirit of God dwells in you?" (1 Corinthians 3:16) My unauthorized translation: There's a sunrise in the heart of every believer!

The day I finally accepted the truth of that verse—that the Holy Spirit Himself has taken up residence inside of me—I began to relinquish my proud control and allow myself to be led into the mystery of the Trinity. I didn't try to understand it, but simply entered with the abandon of a child entering his own home. And why wouldn't I? I was free: "Now the Lord is the Spirit, and where the Spirit of the Lord is, there is freedom" (2 Corinthians 3:17, NIV).

Knowing that He dwells within helped me to stop viewing God as a distant rule maker and to begin embracing Him as a loving, personal God Who has set me free to experience Him in all I do—both at church and home, in the momentous events of life like the birth of a child or the joy of a wedding, and in times of grief, like my grandfather's funeral. Over time I learned that I could even experience Him in the mundane parts of life, like when paying bills, or taking out the trash, or driving in traffic (don't worry, I haven't come unhinged), or taking care of Bob the goldfish whom your son won in a Vacation Bible School contest and who, five years later, still refused to die (Okay, now I'm unhinged). But wait! There is no mundane! It's all exciting when you discover that the inspiration you've sought all your life is everywhere around you and also within you.

I thank the Holy Spirit for showing me this firsthand and for teaching me that every moment of my life is an inspired journey into the heart of a mystery, into the heart of an artist, and into the heart of a friend.

Jesus is my friend. I know Him best as God, Savior, Shepherd, my model for living, but I've made hard work out of knowing Him as a friend. I'm coming around.

Jesus is an all-around great guy and hale fellow well met don't you think? The perfect friend—pleasant company at the ball game, a wonderful fishing buddy (I hear He's rather good at it), a super guy to pal around with, maybe to go camping and stay up late around the campfire roasting marshmallows and telling ghost stories with. And what a kidder He'd be. Can you imagine the comedic timing? Naturally He'd be there during the tough times, too, to help change my flat tire, sit at my bedside when I'm ill or sad. And how fascinating to have a master carpenter as a friend. I'd love to be an apprentice hanging out in His shop, listening to the radio in the background, carving a couple of table legs and shooting the breeze in between. What a pretty picture.

And now that I've painted it, why do I feel a twinge of guilt? Like I've committed some form of blasphemy? I'll answer that. False humility masquerading as guilt. "You need to show more reverence, Brother Murray," it cries out. I let it spin its wheels and then give it what for: "Back down! There's nothing wrong with my picture. Jesus, the God of the universe, pronounced me His friend (John 15:15). You have a problem with that? Take it up with Him." That usually settles the matter.

It should anyway. But I'm a work in progress. I still need to learn to relax more and be myself with Him instead of approaching Him with manufactured deference. I rationalize that He has more important things to do than to play bocce ball and grill out on a Saturday afternoon. But that's not so. Jesus always has the time—He's quite the multitasker you know. No matter the circumstance, He extends to me an open invitation that says, "Let's hang out." That's what friends do. They also lay down their life for their friends (John 15:13).

And so it comes to this, I think: Jesus died for me, then resurrected, and now wants to be my friend. That is a soul-searingly generous offer and there is only one thing I need do: accept Jesus as my friend and allow Him to make way for me to enter the heart of an approving Father.

Tell that to my own heart. I have known God the Father as a supreme, wise, benevolent figure, yet I have struggled to feel His love. When I first knew God, my view of Him as Father was influenced by my own experience with my good, imperfect father—a hard-working, disciplined, humorous, intelligent, regular human being whose approval I wanted to gain. I was intimidated by him even as I chased after him hoping to secure an "attaboy." A normal desire for any child, given that none of us have perfect fathers, but emotional baggage for an adult who doesn't learn to take hold of God as the perfect Father.

I refuse to cry in my milk. We don't get to blame our parents, our DNA, or our environments for our conceptions or rather misconceptions about God the Father. I've been to that pity party before and only one person showed up. The fact that we can know God the Father personally makes the point moot anyway—painful in the temporal, but eternally moot.

Today I can experience that eternity at will because my Heavenly Father reveals Himself as a God of pure love, protection, guidance and care, and yes, even admonition, but also affirmation and joy. He is my Father Who waits in the field searching for the first sign of His prodigal boy, soul-tattered and worn, stripped of pride, returning home to be restored (Luke 15:11-32). That's Who my Father is—the loving God Who through unrestrained tears recognizes me from miles away, Who can't get to me fast enough to wipe the tears from my eyes, clothe me in His best robe, feed me His finest feast, and tell me that He is proud. I am the prodigal come home, and the long-sought reunion with my Father has begun.

———

I am also a newborn lamb on unsteady legs, learning to walk in relationship with the Holy Spirit Who desires to love me and vitalize my relationship with the Father and the Son. Through that love, He shows me how the Trinity relates, all as one perfect loving union, yet with three distinct personalities.

And now I realize that the Trinity is not something I can explain after all. But it is something I feel, which is a deeper knowing. And that is a rote, doctrinal-sounding affirmation if ever I heard one, so let me try again. If I were to describe the picture of what I feel with merely human words, it would look like this: I am a contented child walking freely about my Father's house. I see my adoring Father and run to Him and climb familiarly onto His lap, where I'm loved by the matchless comfort of the Holy Spirit, as I listen to Jesus my friend and Savior share another heartwarming parable about a contented sheep who learns to receive the nurture and love the Good Shepherd always provides.

And friends, that's the best I've got—my feeble foray into the deepest of the deep, and an admittedly incomplete portrayal. I've tried before and I just can't take it all in, or more like get it all out. Perhaps that is the point; I wasn't meant to. I have a better chance of taking in all the oxygen on Earth in a single breath. At least it's finite. This is an infinite mystery from the infinite imagination of the Master Artist Who holds the sunrise in His hands and breathes inspiration into my heart. I guess when it comes down to it, all I really know is I am in His painting, and that is too wonderful for words.

Chapter 14

The Church Tango

I have been a prodigal church congregant.

I wasn't raised in the church environment, so-called. Other than some scattered childhood experiences—a wedding here, a funeral there—I didn't particularly know what went on inside all those pretty white buildings.

One Sunday, one summer, my mom took my brother and me to church. I'm sure she sensed we needed something more than what she or my dad could provide (right she was). That, plus we were undoubtedly "in her hair," or being "pains in the neck" as she would have said, and perhaps the go-to prescribed remedy of sending us outside "to get the ants out of our pants" wasn't working that summer. It proved a foreshadowing day that I've never forgotten, particularly that first Sunday school experience before the service.

I only went once, but I can tell you what I was wearing, where I was sitting, and that I, the newcomer, blissfully naive, yet attentive as all get out, raised my hand to every question posed about our lesson on Noah's ark, as if I even knew. I couldn't get enough. That may not sound like a memorable day, but consider: I was a boy who had a thirst in his heart that nothing at school, home, or playground had ever quenched. You might say something in me had awakened.

Later, as we sat with my mother in the sanctuary, I heard my first sermon and opened the pew Bible (another first) to follow right along with the preacher. I didn't understand much of what he said, other than that it related to why we are all here—the meaning of life. Oh, my soul! And the answer is?

I listened intently for a good hour with nary an ant in the pants. As I studied the preacher, I remember thinking (if not these words, this sentiment): "This standing around talking to people about the meaning of life might be a first-rate job for me." I had already dismissed my other options: quarterback for the Miami Dolphins (a long-shot), ice cream truck driver (hyper competitive), business-man (way too abstract). What is business anyway? You drive off in the morning in a stiff, white collared shirt, then come back home when it's too late or you're too worn out to play outside. I couldn't see the fun in that. But as for this church stuff—count me in.

That first sermon was the last sermon I heard as a child.

The next one that reached my ears was shortly after I became a Christian, when on my first day at church, I looked around the sanctuary at the other congregants and projected onto them the great lives and perfect relationships that I aspired to. "Naturally they have it all together," I thought. "They're in church after all." I learned better. I learned every church has its imperfections and that, as the saying goes, it is not a place for perfect people, or else I wouldn't be allowed in. Imperfect is one thing, not preaching Jesus is another.

Not long after we began attending church number two—the one with the nice, yelling pastor, and the decent, faithful, imperfect people—I noticed that for many of them it was a Sunday thing. The rest of the week was business as usual—their lives, for the most part, mirroring the world—till Sunday rolled around again. Then it was clean up and head on out to assemble and smile for the church compartment of life.

I couldn't tell you how many felt like I did. Granted the Lord knows I did my share of mirroring the world, but He also knows my heart. And I didn't spend thirty-six years seeking the Water of Life only to drink from it once a week, particularly now that I knew it was available to me through God's Spirit around the clock. I wanted to be "all in," wholehearted for God. I knew that was the tougher road, both exciting and frightening to me, but couldn't think of any higher purpose in life, couldn't see any good reason not to be that way. So while I enjoyed a full family life and played businessman on the side, I focused the better part of my days on my faith in God, or rather on studying about Him, naively assuming that that amounted to the same thing.

One thing I got right—I understood that my priority as a father was to introduce my children to God in hopes that they would one day accept Jesus as Savior, which all four did (amen, amen, amen, and amen!) during those early years. My next priority was to give them the best chance to grow in their faith, which to my way of thinking meant being surrounded by others who were "all in" with theirs.

With those well-intentioned motives, I switched to my third imperfect church in three years. The prodigal congregant, on the move again.

If I wanted to find people who were totally committed to their faith, I was not to be disappointed, not in that way at least. Our new church was a much-needed improvement. The environment was a great fit, filled with wholesome, God-loving people and great influences for our children—a place where many of the families lived their faith as a day-in-day-out proposition. Proposition? Yeah, as in, you do your part, hold up your end of the bargain, and then God will be pleased. Uh-oh! I've been here before!

At first I was excited to be rubbing elbows with so many people wholly devoted to their Savior, but soon I realized that, just like the last church, they were by large measures preaching and teaching a works-based approach to their relationship with Him. Every sermon was punctuated with the solicitation to confess, repent, and get back in fellowship with God. Thankfully, I knew by then that by God's grace I already enjoyed an eternal fellowship that would never be broken. However I met a lot of people there who believed it was only God's mercy which precluded their being struck by hurtling lightning bolts and passing from the quick to the dead on a daily basis, figuratively speaking of course; but trying to live that way is slow death for the soul any way you look at it.

In all the years we attended that church, I don't recall hearing a single sermon on God's grace, though I heard countless sermons on the Ten Commandments and on how, although my salvation was eternally secure, my fellowship with God depended upon my daily adherence to those "standards." On second thought, I recant the previous sentence—I heard many sermons on grace. They were my own, spoken with urgency and passion all the way home from church every Sunday, and oftentimes referred to as the sermon after the sermon, or secretly, Dad's redundant rants. And I suppose they were as I deconstructed the theology of the sermon and re-formed it into a message of God's grace, ignoring the promptings of the Holy Spirit to be graceful myself and talking right past a carload of entreaties to stop for lunch, much to the consternation of my family who'd had their fill of me, if not the rules and regulations of church and school.

I didn't like what I was becoming, and my familiar remedy was to dive deeper into my studies on grace, much like a man possessed—in a good way, you see. I was attempting to retrain my mind so the Ten Commandments would stop banging around in my head, figuring I might eventually be able to hear what God was trying to tell my heart, which I believe was to stop preaching and start loving.

To this day, when I pass by a yard with one of those Ten Commandments signs out front, I wince—though it's a wince of compassion more than of criticism, which is progress for me—and I have a private conversation in my mind with the homeowners inside:

"Been coveting lately? Yeah, me too. Keeping the Sabbath without fail? You're better than me, friend. Have any other gods before God? Yes, sports can be a god. Honoring your father and mother? What's that? Usually but…? But nothing. Other than this: we were never meant to keep the law!"

I look forward to the day all these same yards are dotted with signs that read, "Love the Lord your God with all your heart and with all your soul and with all your strength and with all your mind; and, Love your neighbor as yourself" (Luke 10:27, ESV). And that's all.

For hundreds of Sundays I heard persistent sermons by fine men who were on the performance train worse than I was. And here I came to this latest church looking for a way off, only to learn that I was heading down the tracks on the bullet train.

It's not for me to say which of my brothers and sisters were missing the heart of God. All I know is there weren't many preaching or talking about it. Finding a church where I could grow both closer to God and to others was proving elusive. They always looked good from a distance, but every time I moved closer, the vision moved away. Like chasing down that mirage of vapor floating above the hot blacktop highway, I could never quite get there. It was enough to make me think the problem wasn't in the church, but in me.

—⁓—

My kids are grown now, all strong of faith. Despite my prodigal ways, my wife and I accomplished our goal of raising them in the church. We took Hebrew 10:25 to heart, "not forsaking our own assembling together, as is the habit of some, but encouraging one another; and all the more as you see the day drawing near." Through all my fits and starts, I never gave up "assembling together." Wise choice, for through that process I came to understand something vital about my fellow church congregants: Christ is in each of them too!

Even so, I couldn't find in the Bible, or in my heart, an absolute prescription for the form that assembly must take. And that was the snag for me through all my prodigal church years. I worshiped corporately plenty, but trying to connect to the body of Christ through the prism of an organization, denomination, preaching, music style, or for any reason other than to connect directly with the people themselves—the church body—is prodigal lunacy.

I have finally come to my senses and to a different, more relational understanding of church assembly, and no surprise, I love going to church again. I'm learning instead of pulling apart the sermon, to pray for the pastor and listen for the heart of God which is always present within us, even though we may use theologically imperfect words to express it. And I'm learning that going to church isn't a meeting you attend, it's a family you love. And I'm learning (I'm just learning and learning here!) that if the church is the body of Christ and Christ is the head over His church, then that means we don't need to go to a church to be the church. After all, does a Christian prisoner in a foreign land stop being a part of the church body? How about the person who is confined to a hospital bed for an extended time? The elderly who can't leave home? To be sure, the answer is no on every count. They are a part of the church, as we all are, wherever we are, because Christ is in us. And yes, that means even when we aren't assembling!

The beauty and grace of it all is that we *get* to go to church, to spend time worshiping God together and building up one another, not as any sort of obligation, but as a divine privilege, set aside not for the perfect, but for the imperfect who are being transformed in God's time.

Part Three

PADDLING TO NOWHERE

Chapter 15

AWAKE!

*Spirituality is determined not by the type of
activity, but by who is the source of the activity.*

BOB GEORGE,
GROWING IN GRACE

So who am I all these many years since I first accepted Christ,
besides a fidgety congregant and an imperfect philosopher?
Early on I would have told you I am a person who loves Jesus; likes
learning, watching sports, walking the dogs, laughing, parsing,
creating, observing, traveling, reading; and enjoys family, friends,
and a good meal. There's more, but on the whole that sums it up
properly. Alternatively, I might have answered with a list of attributes like thrifty, brave, kind (not my list, but you get the idea); or
perhaps with a list of accomplishments: former kickball enthusiast,
former household ping pong champ, and... and sad to say that's all

I could come up with. But one answer I would not have given is that I am a holy child of God who at his core experiences the fullness of Christ and the fruit of God's Spirit, and who every moment of every day has access to God's power through His unending love.

I was His child all right, but I didn't know the full extent of what that meant in my early walk. It's not that I believed I was the sum of my preferences and attributes. I knew there was more to me—to all of us—than that. But rolling around for years upon years in the grime of the world has a way of soiling perspective and masking the truth of one's identity.

That truth came calling, as earlier shared, on a providential night when I bowed down and asked Jesus to be my Savior. Right away I knew I was different. No bright lights or booming fanfare, just inner light and an enfolding peace. The instant I accepted Christ, who I was had changed. I had a new identity. And although I couldn't explain it then, I certainly felt it.

Regrettably, in less than a year, that feeling was gone, buried and forgotten under a burden of self-effort and Christian performance, of trying to look the part. Things continued in that mode for nearly a decade before God's abundant grace moved from my mind to my heart, or do I have that backwards? Either way, the feeling was a relief, an unburdened rest, and so different from anything I ever learned from the world. The world I knew was a demanding place filled with performances, and none of them were good enough. That's why it never rests. Instead it labors and groans under a global identity crisis, same as it has ever since Adam and Eve unceremoniously exited the Garden of Eden. The only chance for mankind to find their true selves again is by turning back to Jesus, one man at a time.

As I say, I had already turned back and given my life to Jesus and learned that I lived under the fullness of grace. Yet during that decade of self-effort, I still had a big problem. Great gobs of my life looked an awful lot like the world. I knew how to clean up for church and friends—honestly, don't we all?—but inside I knew my private thoughts and behaviors weren't well suited for public consumption. "I thought I'd be a better person by now," rattled in my mind more than once. In retrospect, the fact that it pestered me was an improvement in my condition. It led to the beginning of my awakening from a sort of spiritual amnesia, a progressive awakening that I suppose will take the rest of my life.

And to tell how it began will take some doing and a teeming heap of metaphors, detours, and excess to describe what I've awakened to so far. But first, fair warning. What follows in the chapters ahead is not for those who want to receive credit or earn their way into God's good graces. It is for those who are willing to lay themselves down at the foot of the cross and allow God's love to unslumber their dormant hearts.

Awake, O sleeper.[20]

Chapter 16

A Ghost Story

It always is Christmas Eve, in a ghost story.

Jerome K. Jerome

"I'm just a sinner saved by grace," is the hackneyed, self-effacing refrain. Malarkey sauce! Thanks be to God for leading me to such writers as Charles Solomon and Francois Fénelon, who reminded me that God has a different view:[21] "I have been crucified with Christ; and it is no longer I who live, but Christ lives in me; and the life which I now live in the flesh I live by faith in the Son of God, who loved me and gave Himself up for me "(Galatians 2:20).

So then—deep breath—if my identity is Christ in me, then who is "me"? And my seventh grade English teacher faints, from which I get smug satisfaction and break into the most immature "Nah, nah, nah, nah, nah," then catch myself and ask, "Who is this impudent rascal in here with me?" Clearly there is a huge part of me that wants the best for people—even for my seventh grade English teacher, though not quite so much—yet there is something seriously off-kilter. If Christ is in me, why do I have these ignoble moments of disdain at all? Where's the love?

Perhaps I can't help myself because I'm just a sinner saved by grace. No! No! No! That person no longer lives! That old sinner has been crucified along with Christ. Dead and buried he is. There aren't two of me. I have one life which is Christ in me joined to my new, resurrected spirit. And since God is 100 percent pure good and, as the expression goes, even a single drop of oil makes an ocean of water less than pure, I can rest assured He's not about to taint His purity. My spirit is forever pure, perfect, holy. And that causes me discomfort to write because of false humility again, which is really that old nemesis, pride.

Ah yes! Pride! Because I'm just a sinner saved by grace. Objection! Cease and desist! I am not a sinner at my core. I'm God's child and I'm made to live by the power and purity of God's Spirit in me. Those are the facts. Admittedly, too often I live by my own efforts. But inside I know I'm made to live by faith in Christ, and that He, not I, will live out His life in me by that same faith. "For it is God at work in you, both to will and to work for His good pleasure" (Philippians 2:13). Much better!

Just a sinner saved by grace? Not at all. Just someone who walked around for too long with a bad case of spiritual amnesia. Christ lives in me now, the new me. I have a new identity. Any questions? Only one, Mr. New Identity. If you're so new, then why do you—just like this old world—keep groaning under the weight of your own failings.

I believe I have the sobering retort. Since Jesus offers to carry the weight of my burdens (Matthew 11:28-30), it must be that my failings are the result of my not letting Him.

—◊—

Paul's admission of futility—"I do not understand what I do. For what I want to do I do not do, but what I hate I do" (Romans 7:15, NIV)—used to strike me as both an indecipherable confession and an amusing tongue twister right up there with "She sells seashells down by the seashore," till I did some math.

God is a Creator of infinite variety, an artist of spellbinding beauty, and a mathematician of the highest order, Who delights in working in threes. The Father, Son, and Holy Spirit speaks for Itself (or is it Themselves?). And consider these threes: past, present, future; height, length, width; solid, liquid, gas; The Beatles, the Rolling Stones, the Bee Gees. Okay, the last grouping doesn't fit. However the list is extensive, and includes—aptly for our purposes—man, who is comprised of spirit, soul, and body (1 Thessalonians 5:23).

For much of my Christian life, I succumbed to the worldly-wrong view that I am a tangible body foremost, inhabited by a soul (otherwise known as the personality) that has a spirit somehow undergirding it all. I've since learned I had the order reversed. I am a spirit foremost who has a soul residing within a body. This is what Paul well knew and what led to his entangling words, which if I were to paraphrase, would read: "I want to live according to the Spirit within me, but I keep doing the opposite." Indeed a common frustration, for which I learned there is a holy, life-changing remedy.

To explain what it is, we must begin with a ghost story trilogy:

The Spirit. I learned that my spirit is that part of me where the Holy Spirit resides. Or as author Ian Thomas writes, "The human spirit is that part of us where God lives within us in the person of the Holy Spirit, so that with our moral consent (and never without it), God gains access to our human soul."[22] Wish I had come up with that.

Formerly, my spirit was not God's residence. I was born into this world with a fallen nature and a dead spirit, which I inherited, same as you, from my great, great, great—keep going back hundreds of greats and maybe a couple of not-so-greats till you get to my, rather our, earliest grandfather, Adam, who so happens to be the first man on the planet. When I said "yes" to Christ, God cut out my old dead inherited spirit and gave me a new resurrected one, made up of His perfect Holy Spirit joined to my now unblemished one (1 Corinthians 6:17). Unblemished I say, because it is connected to God and we know already that He would never join with anything less than pure. Thus, at the precise moment of my union, an unbreakable marriage born of grace occurred. A marriage that doesn't depend on me, but on Christ in me. I was possessed. Scared yet?

Before I received Jesus as my Savior, although I was biologically alive ("*bios*" in the original Greek), I was not yet possessed with the eternal life ("*zoe*") of God in me. For that reason, anything I did previously, in that it was motivated from out of my despoiled soul (we'll get to this), even if it looked noble or good from the outside, was ultimately selfishly motivated and nothing more than future ashes. In my fallen state, it couldn't have been otherwise. For when I was a louse at heart my soul was connected to my dead spirit. And what do you suppose it could gain of value from that relationship? Right. Nothing! A corpse makes a bad teacher. Macabre, but true.

And that brings us to the second part of our trilogy.

The Body. Ninety-two years after my grandfather came into this world, he passed away into the next. I kissed him minutes after that happened and immediately wished I hadn't. His body was already cold, which surprised me (They don't tell you that in the movies). I realized at once I was kissing a memory, that he was no longer there.

Unless I'm fated to live beyond a hundred, my body is nearer the end than the beginning. Certainly cheeseburgers and ice cream cones aren't helping my cause. To lighten my consumption guilt, I refer to the quip by the late comedian, Redd Foxx: "Health nuts are going to feel stupid someday, lying in hospitals dying of nothing." It seems no matter what we do to try to stave it off, these bodies will wear out sooner or later.

But humor and cheeseburgers aside, I don't take lightly my responsibility to take care of this body while I have it. It is tempting to rationalize that since I'll get a new body one day, I might as well run this one into the ground—which happens to be where it will end up. However, that is a most selfish line of reasoning, for it ignores Who owns this body, not to mention Who resides in here with me. "Or do you not know that your body is a temple of the Holy Spirit who is in you, whom you have received from God, and that you are not your own?" (1 Corinthians 6:19) In other words, my body is a gift from God. True enough. But still unwise to shout out during the next Bible study class.

I can make the most out of the body I've been given, revel in all it is capable of doing. But since I'm not the one who created it, I have no valid reason to take credit for or to disparage this body, nor to envy or disparage the body God gives to anyone else. I suppose I could have been born in any other body in this world of seven billion varieties, possibly yours. Had that been the case, I likely would have faced many of the same physical challenges you've faced. Yet make no mistake, my spirit and soul would be the same one I have today. The quality, the race, or the look of the body can't alter the fact that I would still be me! The soul has the body, not the other way around. That's how I see it. Scholars may trifle with the finer points of how it all works, but I do believe that's the heart of the matter.

And the challenge of the matter is to respect these bodies as gifts from God without worshiping them as vessels of vanity. Big muscles, fine. Big ego, not so fine. I can steward my body by treating it in the ways God's Word directs, with moderation and respect, watching what goes into it and what I do with it. But I have delusions of grandeur if I worship it or give it a priority it doesn't deserve. One day I'll be "absent from the body" and "at home with the Lord" (2 Corinthians 5:8), and I don't imagine I'll say, "Where's my other body, God? Do you suppose we could get it up here? I spent half my life trying to whip it into shape and we've really grown quite fond of each other." Now if only I lived out the spirit of my conviction.

Recently, after pulling a muscle in my shoulder while raking leaves, in a less than transparent grab for affirmation, I said to my wife, "Wow, my body sure is falling apart." She responded with an even-keeled, "Yeah well, you had a good run." Ouch! I wanted her to deny I was joining the ranks of the infirm, but she's not good at lying. That's one of my strengths, or in this case, one of my vanities.

We are all prone to unrealistic thinking, I suppose—"I'm as good physically as I ever was, and if I'm not, by Jupiter, I'm willing to focus inordinate time and effort trying to be." It's as if we are tethered to these bodies as our statements to the universe. "See me," my pride demands when I'm in some semblance of physical shape (I recollect the feeling). "Quit looking at me," I privately sulk when I've gained holiday weight. It is sadly too common and always misguided that the scale and mirror disproportionately affect my self-esteem. Don't I have the same soul and spirit either way? I can admonish myself for breaking the diet, make efforts to improve even, but shouldn't my self-esteem be unaffected given the proper eternal view?

Regardless of the state of this imperfect body, not to miss is that I am being prepared for something far greater: "Therefore we do not lose heart. Though outwardly we are wasting away, yet inwardly we are being renewed day by day" (2 Corinthians 4:16, NIV).

Simply put, Botox can't compete with gravity and time, and neither can I.

Everyone enjoys looking at beauty, be it a flower, a sunset, or a smiling face. Beauty is a blessing that comes from God, but it is tough on those who have it. Yes, you read that correctly. In the most important sense, all bodies are created equal—they all have equal opportunity to be inhabited by God, their Creator. However, not all bodies look the same. Some look better than others.

Madison Avenue exploits this reality with their shallow world-worn advertising campaigns built on a strong societal impulse that has been afoot for the last, oh, let's say, six thousand years. They all promote an obsession with being attractive, the flaunting of your good looks in order to feel good about life and your place in it. "Look at me! Look at me! Please look at me!" they say. And we reward them by looking—and copying.

All these unconcealed expressions of our vanity have only intensified over the course of my lifetime and it has cost us dearly. Many of the most physically attractive among us are secretly the most miserable as they travel the narcissistic roads of the world and drink the poison of their false identity. While society extols them for what only God can give, it becomes all too easy to confuse their good looks with the value of their soul and to miss the true loving purpose for which God gave them their lives to begin with. "Look at me, you throngs of mere averageness" is a recipe for loneliness in the middle of the largest crowds.

—⟋⟍—

M y friend Pete Hudson was a kind Christian man with a beautiful spirit and a love of horses. Toward the end of his battle with cancer, his wife drove him over to see my newly-constructed barn—a beginner's version of what he had built. I knew he was really there to say goodbye. I was taken aback when I saw him. Burly Pete with the gentle soul was now frail and gaunt, barely recognizable. Too weak to get out of the car, he sat quietly, contentedly, while surveying the barn. As I stood next to him, enjoying the peaceful silence of friendship for a good ten minutes, out of his frail body drawled the familiar, soothing timbre that could put babies to sleep. "It's nice," was all he could muster (I believe he meant more than the barn). This he followed with an accepting smile that meant, "Don't worry. I'll be okay, pal." Then he and his wife left.

On that brief visit he was somehow more "Pete" than ever. A few weeks later he was dead. Rather, his body was.

Chapter 17

THE PADDLING FOOL

Before I formed you in the womb I knew you.

JEREMIAH 1:5

To complete our ghost story trilogy, we now turn to the soul.

<u>The Soul</u>. I used to be a paddling fool, literally. Many days I'd paddle my yellow canoe across a large serene pond, starting out appreciably to enjoy the tranquil surroundings—the fresh air, the geese, the fish, the water bugs skating with their hands clasped behind their backs—all with the added bonus of a bit of leisurely exercise thrown in. Yet it often unfolded spectacularly differently. I'd spend most of the time working myself sweaty sore (I'm competitive that way), then finding some problem to worry about (any problem would do). And usually at some point, boredom would ooze in, until finally, one too many mosquito bites later,

I was nothing more than one of the many ill-tempered denizens fighting to survive this sweltering microbial sinkhole! All of a sudden I couldn't get away fast enough. So much for tranquility. What happened? Would the real me please stand up? Or in this case, paddle?

The *real me* is right here, once again thanking my brother Paul, this time for helping me realize that a real me actually exists. Like him, "I do not understand what I do" either. But then again, I do: "So now, no longer am I the one doing it, but sin which dwells in me" (Romans 7:17).

I am not overstating when I say that when the words "sin dwells in me" finally sank in, it was a life-changing revelation. Turns out there are not two natures fighting inside of me like I had been taught, for I only have one nature to start. And it's fighting—I should say, I'm fighting—not against myself, but against sinful flesh ("*sarx*" in Greek). Sin dwells in me! Clearly that sin is not living in my spirit since God is there to ensure that never happens. Which means, then, that the sin is taking up residence in my soul. And that explains a lot about my inconsistent behavior, all of it in fact.

Take as an example my aforementioned pond meltdown. At the start I had every intention of being the "peaceful man of leisure" out enjoying the bounteous day. I know this is true because I would have pressed the "red button" to make it so. What's more, every Christian to whom I've ever given my "red button test" has responded the same way. And you're wondering right now what in Casper's name a red button has to do with our ghost story.

To better explain what I'm getting at, I will paraphrase a recent conversation I had with a friend who confided in me, "I'm just an impatient person." After telling him I shared his problem—it is one of my endearingly vexing traits—the following was my response (note: the names have been changed to protect the not-so-innocent, and I've enhanced my side of things so as to appear more astute than normal; other than that it's all true):

"So if I have this straight, this matter of impatience is causing you all kinds of grief and you've concluded it's just the way you are. Let me describe a hypothetical scenario to see if it's really true that you are, at the core, an impatient person.

"Imagine you and your all-American family are driving in the car and you're running late for little Billy's soccer game. The man in the car in front of you is simultaneously texting, eating a doughnut, and looking at his perfect hair in the mirror, all at a rolling speed which you notice has failed to keep pace with the elderly gentleman shuffling along at turtle speed on the sidewalk next to you. You accurately conclude you're going to miss the traffic light as a result, the five minute variety.

"Do you, A) Take a few deep breaths and think to yourself, 'I'm okay with this. It's such a lovely day and now I'm blessed to sit here with God for five more minutes to take it all in,' B) Take those same breaths and press the horn ever-so-slightly, hoping for the polite version of a beep so as not to come across as an impatient person, or C) Skip the breaths and lay into the horn with all you've got because you, in a flash, think about how this ignoramus is about to make you late to the game, which means Billy will get demoted to bench, resulting in his missing out on that scholarship you've been counting on—which no one besides you thinks is forthcoming in a million years anyway—but you calculate this matter nevertheless and conclude it will cost you a great deal of money which so happens to equal the price of that new bass boat you've been eyeing?

"If it is C—and we both know it is, friend—perhaps your next move is a contemptuous raising up of both hands followed by a succession of red-faced huffs, not to mention a few under-your-breath choice words, all less than becoming of your position as an elder at the local church. Till suddenly, like all the other times, you come to your senses and hope beyond hope that your coarse actions were visible only to the offending driver. But it is too late! Unfortunately little Billy has seen, and now you realize your lovely wife has seen and is considering sending you various gestures of her own but settles on staring daggers instead. And the day goes downward from there."

I concluded with my friend, "If what I'm describing is in the vicinity of an actual representation of your impatience issues, and if you knew that by pressing an imaginary red button on the table in front of you, God would instantly make a permanent transformation in your soul, removing forevermore the impatient habits within you, would you press that button?"

"Yes!" he shouted at once, rather impatiently I thought. He didn't take a nanosecond to consider his bass boat, but just slammed his hand down on the table where he imagined the button to be.

He even looked surprised and somewhat disappointed there wasn't a button there. I kind of was too.

To recount that conversation was admittedly the long way through, but necessary to emphasize a point. I believe there is a simple reason every Christian to whom I've ever asked this question, as it relates to any flaw or immoral behavior they acknowledge is a struggle, has said, "Absolutely! Where's the button?" And it is this: As Christians they have a new holy identity, and therefore any immoral thoughts or behaviors are no longer natural, but instead have become contemptible stumbling blocks to the new life they know they were created to live.

I can pick any one of my failings and wouldn't hesitate. Would you? I ask because I know we have that choice. There is a red button. In biblical terms it's called "abiding in Christ."

Stay with me. The climax of our frightening trilogy is upon us.

I do not claim to be an expert viticulturist, but I have grown six robust grape vines. Two vine rows of three plants each constitutes a vineyard in my book and qualifies me as rank amateur, from which vantage point I have made two penetrating observations. 1) A branch doesn't produce the grapes, the life-force to do that comes from the vine which is attached through its root stalk to the nutrients of the ground, and 2) A branch that is no longer connected to the vine is dead. It's called a stick.

Jesus says, "I am the vine, you are the branches; he who abides in Me and I in him, he bears much fruit, for apart from Me you can do nothing" (John 15:5). Not only is that infinitely more potent than my mortal words above, it is also a better illustration than my red button one, don't you think?

"To abide" in the context of this verse means "to remain," or "to rest," in complete dependency. It's what a branch is made to do and it doesn't have to work to do it. To the contrary, it takes work to pull away. When I rest my soul in the Spirit of God within me, a whole host of good things happen; chiefly, virtues known as the fruit of the spirit are produced by God. My privileged role is to bear them. Galatians lists this fruit as love, joy, peace, patience, kindness, goodness, faithfulness, gentleness, and self-control (5:22-23). Not a bad day's produce.

So taking my cue from Jesus' own words, it is clear why so often, like Paul, "What I want to do I do not do," or put another way, why I cease to bear fruit: I stop resting in Jesus. It has nothing to do with the false notion I often hear that there are two natures fighting within me ("Just feed the good nature and starve the bad and you'll be fine"). That bad advice isn't in Scripture, and is merely another version of "Pick yourself up and try harder."[23] I've tried to do that countless times and it doesn't work, nor was it ever supposed to. I have one nature—Christ in me—and the battlefront isn't me against myself. It is me against indwelling sin—the flesh. And I won't ever conquer that enemy apart from Christ.

In my heart I agree with everything that I've written here. In my actions, I repeatedly fail to live it out, too often ignoring my true identity. Whenever I do, in no time flat I grow restless. Next

I try to double my efforts, and soon after that I'm barren as a twig. All these failures are predictable, frustrating, and born from a lack of trust, really. Yet I know they no longer define me. God defines me. And understanding that truth moves me closer to His heart, where I find a love that encourages me to a winning formula—trust God and let go of everything that's not rest. Simple, profound, and the only man who could ever do it perfectly was Jesus. Hence I journey on.

———

And to our mutual cheer, our unconventional ghost tale has come to an end. I've paddled, pressed some buttons, picked grapes, and learned that I had been possessed all the while. Frightening, wasn't it? Well, perhaps not. Although I admit this journey through life feels frightening at times, even as my growing faith tells me there is no need to fear.

Nowadays when I paddle across the pond, I'm aware of the astounding miracle that Jesus goes with me. Better yet, without exception, He offers to do all the paddling. And I'm learning to let Him. That might sound lazy to the uninitiated who miss the distinction that I still hold the oar, pull through the water, sweat, and feel the burn, even though it is Jesus Who animates my thoughts and actions as I travel along. It is a peaceful way to journey.

At least it is until an old meddlesome impulse rises up: "Since I'm holding the paddle, Jesus, I might as well take over from here."

I suppose the disciple Peter thought something similar when he tried to walk on water apart from Jesus, right before he began to sink.

To experience the presence of Jesus in a more continually restful way is the longing of my soul, but for crying out loud! this indwelling sin is a stubborn mule. Praise God that by His Word I am now well acquainted with how to right myself—I simply choose to depend again on His love and power within me. I abide. And though still my muscles ache and the mosquitoes bite—the cost of living in a fallen world—when Jesus paddles through me, it is worth the while.

As I think of that now, I breathe a sigh of relief and stop paddling in my mind. And a pleasing image comes to view, reminding me that one day my life here will end, and I will get a new body that will never ache, and my soul will live on happily ever after.

To quote my friend Pete, "It's nice."

Chapter 18

SOUL MAN

I've met some charming personalities in my day, and some decidedly threadbare ones (you know who you are). Most of us fall somewhere in-between and bebop along in the vast middle-lands with the rest of the average schmoes. Fine by me. In God's eyes there's nothing average about any of us. We're all one-of-a-kind, made in God's image, and created to live out the life of Christ within us—a life of unceasing contentment and relational excellence, and brimming with love. Pretty outstanding, that.

Now the bad news—we're not there yet. All of us are flawed and need to change. Yes, even the personable sorts among us have these same pervasive flaws, some worse. I don't know anyone who has it all together. You didn't think I did, did you?

—⚬⚬⚬—

As I continued in the forward direction of my faith, I came to understand my identity is "Christ in me," joined to my spirit. I accepted that my waning body was not destined, no matter the effort, to defy entropy. And I had come to the inescapable conclusion that all my flaws, so desperately in need of transformation, reside in my soul in the form of indwelling sin. This last bit was the greatest of news, for at least I knew now where the hammer must strike, and not to mention that it will happen. "For those whom He foreknew, He also predestined to be conformed to the image of His Son" (Romans 8:29). Predestined! One day, after however many hammer strikes, my soul will have it all together.

In my stubbornness, it was hard to see that reality early on. However, thankfully, God has a keen desire that I overcome my lapses and resistance. I'm sure that's why He gave me a desire to pursue truth. I see it as the first step toward change. And it was with that frame of mind that I began to research the Bible to learn the truth about the human soul, hoping this would lead mine to become more yielding in God's hands.

As a consequence, today is your lucky day. You have the dubious privilege of bearing witness to what I've learned about the soul so far. Best of all, we both get to travel merrily further into the fascinating realm of threes. For by God's design, every human soul is comprised of mind, will, and emotions—the triumvirate of the personality. And if you ever meet anyone with four parts, let me know.

<u>The Mind</u>. In my mind, I imagine, think, sort things out, get confused, and sort them out some more. I store up memories, some near and clear, many fuzzy and remote—the good and the confusing of long ago growing up in Miami come to mind.

In my mind, I dream of the future, though usually not big enough or important enough because I use my mind to worry more than dream. But the reality remains: I have the mind of Christ (1 Corinthians 2:16). That means I have capabilities far beyond my propensity to think little thoughts or dwell on earthbound worries. It is not my brain I speak of here; it is far more. The brain is merely the thinking apparatus, a miracle of the body. The mind on the other hand is made to be eternal, and grasps things beyond facts, calculations, or temporal states.

All my life I asked, "Who am I?" Today in my mind I answer, "Christ in me." So what do I want? What Christ wants. And I can barely get those words out before the world scoffs. Let 'em. As already stated, it is my new nature—I have access to what Jesus wants me to know. And I will savor that regardless of the small-minded who want to chop me down to temporal size. Pardon my frustrations for showing. Perhaps you feel like I do—tired of trying to keep your head lower than the world's.

I might behave in ways I don't like, make wrong choices, think wrong thoughts, but I can never in my heart of hearts want something that would be opposed to Christ. And that is a stunner because the logical conclusion, then, is that I can do whatever I want. I throw out the challenge: "In that case, I want to eat a half-gallon of ice cream (it's a fixation with me)," to which I instantly respond with full conviction, "No I don't, that's just indwelling sin talking. That's my flesh. Christ in me wants no such thing, for it would be harmful to me." And I press the red button.

It can be difficult to keep all these distinctions straight, so I've learned to restate the logical conclusion in its truest form: *In my right mind* I can do whatever I want. And when I am not in my right mind, I am in desperate need. That's why I'm thankful God is changing the way I think. Most of my life I've used my mind as a tool for selfish purposes. Often I still do, even though as a Christian I don't want to anymore.

Who am I to argue?

The Will. It has often been said that there are none so blind as those who refuse to see. Several years ago, I listened as a friend tried to convince his sister of the existence of God. It was quite the kerfuffle. He was a believer, she was not, and after a long, heated discussion, seemingly getting nowhere, he saw into the heart of the matter and asked:

"If there were an all-loving, all-powerful God Who had your best interests at heart, would you put your life in His hands?"

"There isn't one," she responded.

"*If,*" he repeated with emphasis.

"No!" She got right to the point. "I wouldn't. I like making my own decisions."

With that, his jaw dropped, the clash of wills was resolved, and the matter was ended, heartbreakingly for my friend.

In the predawn days of learning I was on journey into the heart of God, I knew that something or Someone transcendent beyond this material world of space and time was my only hope. I was lost. Day after day, so lost, to the point where life and death were not opposites, but two sides of the same meaningless mirror of the soul. The moment I knew Jesus as my Savior, the scales came off, life was instantly meaningful, and with great moral clarity, I could declare the death side of things as "bad" and the life side as "good." It's the way I wanted it in my heart, and I surrendered my will to make it so. Until that moment, I could never see that giving my will over to God was in my best interests. I eventually got there, but for reasons I'll never understand, apparently some souls will never have an interest. God desires them and calls for them by name and still they ignore His voice.

Not so fast! I rein myself in. In some sense I do understand. It's the same thing I do every day when it comes to following God's plans for my life. I pick and choose which of His ideas I'm willing to follow, even though I've experienced that He knows best and has the power to bring it about. French theologian and writer Francois Fénelon spoke directly to this. "What do you fear? Finding a God too good to love? A God that will so enamor you that you will not want earthly possessions and the things of this world?"[24] Yes, it must be said—I do!

Living consistently in the heart of God would be joy inexpressible, yet in times of my worst behavior, I exercise my God-given freedom to ignore Him, get mad at Him, and to walk straightaway from His desires for me. Meanwhile, in keeping with His character of unconditional love, He waits for me to return and to allow Him to walk me right back to His heart. He does so not by promising to make my life pain-free but by promising always to give me the better life. It is a fait accompli. I am His child, predestined to be conformed. Ultimately, I will always come to my senses.

Ingrained in me and every believer is the desire *not* to be God. Yet I do like to claim the throne. "I'll take it from here, God," I say once He's solved my latest looming crisis. Or, "Yes, You're my Lord over everything, God. It's all Yours, but not the fun stuff. Not my TV. Not the food or the clothes or the impulse purchases or the sex. Not work or home. Not rest or play. But everything else is all Yours, not counting relationships. Now fix me."

I'm sick and tired of it to the point of reforming any day now. To give Him everything is my overarching desire. And I have done so over and over. I have often been broken about my weakness and lack of commitment, or so I thought. At the very least, I know I've cried the same "take it from me, Lord" prayers till I'm blue in the face. And I have summarily turned around and made the same mistakes all over again.

It's not that I haven't had successes. In key ways He has substantially changed me, but always only after I surrender my will. Then after a while, usually a short one, He'll show me new aspects and parts of my will I haven't trusted Him with. Some I already know about and some are surprises, but always there's another hill to ascend. It's a process, and I know He loves me too much not to take me on that soul-rending climb. So I relent and lay my will down—"Not as I will but as You will, God"—as many times as I need to. To be willing to be willing (not a typo) is the precursor to change. And whenever change comes, I always wonder why I waited so long. In my best moments I see He is God and I am not. That's when I don't hesitate.

My will isn't bad, just broken. After all, it was my will that relented and accepted Christ as Savior. It was my will that followed Him into ministry contrary to the math. It is my will that behaves nobly when my flesh doesn't want to, and I could go on. But there is a part of me—an indulgent, fleshly part—that still holds back in fear that there will be pain, or that I will lose my kind of fun, or that if I fully trust, I will lose me. That's the best way I can explain it. Or maybe this is: It feels a lot like indwelling sin hiding from God in the faithless parts of my soul and prodding me to hide as well.

So the question is always the same: Am I willing to show myself? I'm willing to be willing. I know that much.

In the end it is all so encouraging to me and my uniquely average personality. It is faith-affirming evidence that I have the mind of Christ and that I am already being nurtured toward maturity. I realize that its fulfillment won't happen this side of Heaven, and I accept that because I'm willing to wait.

The Emotions. Of the three facets of the soul, the emotions of man are the most discombobulatingly uncooperative of the bunch—or maybe that's just me.

When I was fifteen, I went to see the now-iconic film *Jaws*, a movie about a monster shark with an inclination to propel itself out of the sea at unsuspecting moments, pretty much in my direction. Twice during the show I nearly unseated myself, and one time I did, jumping into the lap of an elderly woman three rows back if I'm remembering correctly, which of course I'm not.

Maybe my memory is off a smidge on the details, but the fact remains that my emotions were on heightened alert over the specter of that shark for weeks afterward, and I lived well inland! I couldn't shake it then, and I'm sure I never have. I can fancy myself a stoic creature of logic who rises above the realm of pedestrian emotions. But that would be a lie.

There's simply no use trying to escape human emotions. Even when we think we're being logical, they will always have the final say. Consider this from comedian Steve Martin's stand up act from days of yore:

"It's so hard to believe in anything anymore. I mean, it's like, religion—you really can't take it seriously because it seems so mythological; it seems so arbitrary. But, on the other hand, science is just pure empiricism, and by virtue of its method, it excludes metaphysics. I guess I wouldn't believe in anything anymore if it weren't for my lucky astrology mood watch."

Religion? Nope! Science? Don't be silly. But a watch that monitors emotional moods? Gotta have it!

I've been the opposite way for too long—religion and science have been core comforts, while my emotions have been keeping their safe distance, a lot like these birds on my back porch are doing at the moment. And although I'm still considerably more comfortable in the realm of thoughts and ideas than feelings, I have recently come to a consequential insight: I am much more a creature of emotion than logic. Who'da thunk it? I am made to feel! Love, joy, peace, anger, sadness. These emotions and scores of others roam about my soul and connect me to everything else. I see it now. Without them, man would be little more than an imaginative robot who happens to breathe.

"The unexamined life is not worth living," declared Socrates. Turns out neither is the unfeeling one, though in practice I behave mostly as if that doesn't apply to me. My tendency is to think through my feelings rather than feel them, which is the ultimate in gall and pretense, not to mention cowardice. Who am I to hide? My God is the God of great emotions and the Author of mine, and I was created to experience every one of them from the good to the sad.

The great joy of eternal life awaiting God's children was brought about by a loving Son Who followed His Father's desires. The Father sacrificed His Son and experienced untold sadness to ensure a great harvest of souls will enter that eternal life. And the Holy Spirit is here now in the body of Christ to spread the good news until Jesus brings that harvest home. The good and the sad will end in the good.

When I remember that, I laugh and cry with God and I am grateful. I have hope, and walk in peace in the midst of a rejecting world. And through it all I yearn to be where there will be no more sadness ever again. A full gamut of emotions, and all novel experiences for me.

Yes, I am a spiritual infant when it comes to these emotions, and I know why. All my life I built up emotionless defenses to protect myself, knowing that if I ever acknowledged my hidden emotions, all my self-preserving barriers would crash around me and I'd be exposed—to feeling sorrow, mostly, that I wasn't in a better world. Although other painful emotions qualified as well.

All these years later, even as a believer, often instead of coming to God with the pain of these human emotions, I run from Him. Left alone to deal with them in my flesh, I try to push them away. But that only results in a variety of ungodly emotions popping up instead. Fear comes to mind. I let fear guide my decisions, ignoring the prescription to "be anxious for nothing" (Philippians 4:6). Or if it's not fear, often it's despair or envy or shame or insecurity. Need I go on? Oh, it's an ugly thing!

There is only one thing worse. My defenses have made it harder to feel the joy. For as long as I can remember, I've been afraid that if I felt joy too much, it might leave me again. Then I would miss it so deeply that I'd be crushed. Better not to feel it in the first place. I'll ask again: You didn't think I had it all together, did you? My whole emotional strategy is off the rails. At least I know that it's the wrong way through, that it's the short view. I'll give me that.

If I'm to keep growing into spiritual maturity, I can't pretend my emotions don't exist or that they simply do their own thing apart from me. I have to take responsibility and concede every single one of them to God. It's high time to rely on Christ in me to guide me through the full experience of emotions and to teach me to put the immature ones in their proper place. Along with my mind and my will, my emotions are to be, at the very least, an equal part of me, not a remote vestige. I can't love God and love others without them; won't know joy unless I'm willing to risk pain; will never sustain happiness unless I allow myself to feel sorrow. The soul was made to be integrated, and my emotions were made so that I would feel.

I have faith that Jesus, the perfectly emotional Son of God, will carry me past these markers of my fallen past. Today, I'm having a good day and I'm moving forward again, again—with optimism. Life echoes hope, and "God causes all things to work together for good to those who love God, to those who are called according to His purpose" (Romans 8:28). When I'm cheerful, I sing to the Lord. When I'm downcast, I say "Lord, I don't understand, but I believe you'll make it good again." When I have faith, I persevere. And when I hope, I'm at my best.

Tapping into my emotions gives me the capacity to feel all the good ones that God offers and that I have missed all this time. Though I feel sometimes like I'm emptying a pool by the thimbleful, I'm willing to feel it; that's the main thing. And if I will allow myself to fully feel, imagine what could be in store—oceans of love, forests of joy, and skies of peace! Who knows what doors might burst open? Inspiration and passion and beauty and art and all the other endowed aesthetics of life. These are just for starters.

For in the end, man's emotions are messengers of God's greatest truths. They are not meant to be birds on the back porch. They are sonnets of the soul bestowed for the purpose of communing with God and celebrating His goodness in all things.

—ɯ—

The soul is a three-petaled flower. It pollinates with truth, offers its vulnerability, and captivates with beauty. The desire of my soul is one day to effortlessly merge these in such a way that it ignites a flame so huge in me that it burns literally out of my control, until my passion for God consumes me. And that scares me to death.

Part Four

BREAKING THROUGH

Chapter 19

CHOCOLATE LABS AND LIGHTLESS MOONS

Terrified, mortified, petrified, stupefied by you.

JOHN NASH,
A BEAUTIFUL MIND[25]

*The moon doesn't produce light, but
reflects the sun. It is lightless by itself.*

EMPIRICAL OBSERVATION

I have a Labrador retriever whose devotion exceeds that of any dog I've had. If I get up to go to the kitchen for a glass of water, he insists on pushing up from his comfortable spot by my chair and following me. I try to spare him the trouble by saying, "It's okay, boy, wait here, Ill be right back," but I might as well be telling him to hold his breath. He just sighs, long and full—his signal that he has no other choice but to follow me. It is his manifest destiny. So off we go single file into the kitchen, where immediately he plops back down on the floor, just so he can be near to me for a few more precious seconds of his precious life.

I step over him one minute later to make my way back to the den, and his routine repeats. As he's gotten older, he lets out more of a protest groan than a sigh. "Why are you making me do this?" it means, but dutifully, always, he rises to follow—dee-doop-dee-doop. He'll do this as many times as I decide to leave the room. I've tested it.

When I'm not tripping over him, my intuitive reaction is to feel sorry for him, though I shouldn't. He lives to keep his eyes on me, to simply be in my presence. That makes him happy, and his nonstop adoration pleases me to no end. It downright melts my heart.

I could tell of other lessons I've learned from my single-purposed dog, but they all amount to the same thing: complete devotion. That's unquestionable, although I am aware his ability to love has limits. He is a dog after all, a good one, who knows I'm his ticket to table scraps, not to mention for shelter and clothing if you count his collar. Even so, I have a sign on my refrigerator: "I wish I were as good a person as my Lab thinks I am." It helps me keep my life in focus.

I have a sign in my heart that does the same thing. It says: "I wish I were as devoted to Jesus as my Lab is to me."

The Bible says, "God is love," and, "We love, because He first loved us" (1 John 4:16,19). Therefore it follows: God is the source of all love, His character radiates love, and without Him there would be no love anywhere, anyhow, anytime.

Some with a skeptical bent try to reassign this love we humans feel to nothing more than an evolutionary mechanism triggered to ensure survival of the species. To them the origin of love is pinging atoms.

Conversation in an atheist household:

Tommy: Do you love me, Father?

Father: Sure do, Tommy. I'm experiencing an elevated chemical brain reaction right now. I'd give it about a five—not quite as high as yesterday when you cleaned your room. But I'm having it, sure enough.

Kind of gets you right in the ol' breadbasket, doesn't it?

Others who leave God out of the equation dilute the concept of love by confusing it with a lot of substitutes that by themselves won't ever fill the role: infatuation, affinity, service, kinship, companionship, and, we cannot forget, sex—which in godless form translates to "What have you got that I want?"—all come to mind.

The confused set among us manufacture a counterfeit feeling from their inclinations and call it love. But this is just self-interest in a mask. "The one who does not love does not know God, for God is love" (1 John 4:8). How could they? You can't conjure love out of thin air. A flame needs its oxygen. And man's heart needs God if he is to love well; rather, if he is to love at all.

I don't intentionally avoid the love God has for me. I know better than to do that. But I do hide near the edges of its shadows a lot. From there it's hard to feel the enormity of God's love. That's why I don't love well. Simple deduction. Yet I am not discouraged. My journey into God's heart is ultimately as inexorable as my Lab's need to keep me in his sights. It is my natural inclination as God's child to receive His love and radiate it back out, and I will follow Him through all eternity for that blessed purpose. But I'm in the present where my devotion is fickle and I smother my love with the excuses I carry with me. I long to love God more, but how can I love Him when I'm still so broken? How can I love Him when I feel unworthy? How can I afford to love anything? For it would lay my soul bare.

Fickle soul come out to the light! You fool me not!

I read the beautiful passage on love in First Corinthians and realize it not only confers my destiny, it describes God's essential nature. He is all the enumerated aspects of love and more. As I come to know His heart, He will soften and conform mine. Oh, and how I need for His love to shape me till I put Him first, others next. I go last. And now I see the light—I resist the shaping I need because I well know that therein lies the ultimate demise of my flesh. I know because I feel it squirming every time I can't be first.

For those stretches of time when I come out to the light and allow myself to love and be loved, my experiences prove that love is its own reward, love is a worthy risk.

That's what makes marriage such a big step. Though you wouldn't know it based on the cavalier attitude of so many who view selecting a spouse as a child's game of pin the tail on the don-key. Close the eyes of the soul and hope for the best. But love in a marriage is no game; it is holy union and it asks for great sacri-fice—the ultimate price of love I hear (see John 3:16 for confirma-tion). We gladly pay until it asks some unbending part of our flesh to die. Then begins the real struggle.

I have my good moments in loving my wife and others, and I have my struggling moments. Overall I'm annoyingly inconsistent. Worse, I seem to fail the most at being loving to those closest to me. I would run into a burning building to save my wife, yet so often I struggle with the basics of being patient or kind to her. There's a deep-seated love that exists in me, yet in-between heroic feats, where does it go? I trade it away for selfish gain, that's where. And there are more of those times than any soul can keep up with. Sure I'll save her from a burning building, just don't ask me to help with the groceries during the ballgame.

We know the ultimate expression of love between husband and wife is sexual union. It bonds and unites a love that is already deep in their souls. It is a beautiful gift from God. But we all can see how the sex that is being promoted in the world twists that purpose and builds on the temptations of counterfeits. People are beguiled with the fallacy that sex is love. Absent God they are wrong. This is lust of the flesh, nothing more. Their reach is lower than they think. Think underworld low, where the ultimate price is always steeper than the fleeting distraction. And this lust of the flesh comes in many forms, not just sex. Once any of us fall prey, Satan is no longer the tempter, he's the tormentor, and will use what he can to divert our eyes from the true love of God.

I once heard this elegant counter to the enemy's lie from the gifted preacher Adrian Rogers: "Lust is the best thing in this world, but it is not the best thing offered to us."[26] Which I thought was rather lovely.

"I am the way, and the truth, and the life," Jesus says (John 14:6). And His words open my eyes. I can no longer play the child and put on that I don't know the way to God's heart or what I find when I dwell there. I find Jesus. So I have come to a big-boy conclusion: instead of griping, "Why don't I love more? Or feel the love of God more?" I need to take the first step of growing more in love with Jesus. And the way that happens is the same way I grow in my relationship with anyone—by spending time with them. I'm talking Labrador retriever time; anointing Jesus' feet time (Luke 7:37-40).

And epiphany of epiphanies, I will learn to love others and receive the love of others in direct proportion to how much time I spend in intimate relationship with Jesus. This I accomplish through prayer, meditating on His Word, fasting from the buzz of the world, listening for His voice, walking with Him when I'm alone, and walking with Him when I'm with others. In short, learning to abide in Him in everything I do. Or as Brother Lawrence, the seventeenth-century Carmelite monk, called it, "practicing his presence."[27]

Today I take heart that through all the valleys of my inconsistencies I will eventually reach the summit. One day, every day I will experience love in its purist forms: "Love is patient, love is kind. It does not envy..." (1 Corinthians, 13 NIV) Love goes on and on. And God, the Lover of lovers, is all of these; and we, His beloved children, are becoming them. It is inevitable, for love never fails. Just ask my Lab.

Chapter 20

FRIENDLY RELATIONS

*And at the sound of the trumpet, when the
men gave a loud shout, the wall collapsed.*

JOSHUA 6:20 (NIV)

Everyone's got a little crazy in them.

THE SUCCINCT WORDS OF MY WIFE

In an episode from the 1960s sci-fi television classic *The Twilight Zone*, actor Burgess Meredith portrays an introverted bookworm who hates the crush of society and has no need for his fellow man. After a nuclear holocaust he finds himself the only person left on the planet. Certain he has found his Shangri-La, he makes his way through the rubble of the Metropolitan Public Library, a place filled with the idols of his heart—rows and rows of books that would take lifetimes to read. In the closing scene he has gathered together a sizable collection of books. As he sits down on the concrete steps in front of the building to begin his reading marathon, he inadvertently dislodges the glasses from his face which then fall to the ground and shatter, irreparably, along with his dreams. The camera slowly pans away from a pitiable half-blind man, weeping and stumbling about. Fade out. Seems he was wrong.

Being alone on this planet might seem pleasant to some retiring types, but be forewarned, it leads to despair. And madness. Prisoners in isolation are the first of the incarcerated to go crazy (of course they had a head start). Chess players go mad, spending hours by themselves moving pieces of conquest on a square board of right angles, all in silence but for breathing (I like chess). Artists go mad for similar reasons of isolation I think (I like to paint). Proportionately, not as many people go mad who like hanging out with their buddies talking about last night's ballgame (I like this too, so that must be what keeps me sane).

I like people, always have—apart from the one kid who lived down the street in my old childhood neighborhood whose only crime was a continuously runny nose, but that was fifty years ago and I'd like to think perhaps he's changed—although I am an introvert in many ways. As a child I had plenty of friends, boys and girls. The girls were great befuddling fun, and the boys usually became my fast friends, meaning we bonded, which entails a host of proprieties, including no expressed feelings allowed. You play "kill the man with the ball" and get a little blood on you, so what? We're too tough to notice or care. Of course Jesus was tough and also had the tenderest of feelings, but that's an inconceivable balancing act for young tough guys, pretend ones at that. Such was the start of my relating to non-family others.

In those first wobbly steps of building relationships, there were a lot of unspoken rules and expectations that over time became a burden for an introvert at heart who was trying to make way in an extroverted world. Though I don't think I saw myself as an introverted type then. I wouldn't have prized that.

As I grew up, I learned to pretend to go along with the world's expectations—which seemed the best strategy for all concerned— but I always held back the most authentic parts of me, just in case there was more to life than what the world presented. Come to find out there was. But by the time I knew that, I had already built a thick wall between me and a world I didn't truly believe in anyway; built ostensibly so I could get through life safely, minimally scathed—until I could figure out why I was really here in this manifestly broken place. Even after I had accepted Christ, my defensive approach to life had the unintended consequence of sealing vital parts of me behind what had become a wall of isolation. That is, till God used a friend to knock it down.

As an introvert, I didn't mind my wall all those years. But then again, I did. Like I say, I like people. And probably I'm a touch mad.

One of the painfully finest parts of my spiritual growth took place at the men's Bible study group we formed at our workplace.

I looked forward every Wednesday to the lively banter, the fun-loving jabs, and mostly talking about our faith, which to me meant long debates over doctrine, semantical quibbling, and offering—before being asked—my two cents' worth on the finer points of living the Christian life. Sounded like swell company, didn't I? It passed me by that we were to be enjoying fellowship together. I was too busy having a shootout at the O.K. Corral and trying not to end up one of the dead guys face down in the dust. I hadn't learned yet that talking about faith is sharing the love of our Father together. I treated it more like being on the high school debate team, which for sanity's sake, I was never on.

In all, as I was safely situated behind my wall, with logic and debate as my six-guns, it was good fun, apart from the times I ended up in a heap of dust. I couldn't understand why they weren't enjoying it as much. Clearly I was confused about what I was doing and had no clue what God was doing either. I thought I was promoting an initiative within our company to create an environment where we could minister among men—so professional and spiritual-sounding, so misguided. I hadn't yet realized I was the one being ministered to.

After ten years of this, Rob, my business partner at the time, and dear friend still, who is naturally more relational and extroverted than I, put me on the spot one day, and it changed the trajectory of my life. A few days earlier, I had shared with him in confidence a relational struggle I was going through. Now here we were at our men's group and he breached the unspoken protocol of the group (or maybe it was just my protocol): "Kevin, why don't you tell everyone about your struggle you shared with me?" There was more tact, but the words were to that effect.

I clenched my jaw and looked at him with my stoic angry face. Unfazed, he looked right back and repeated his question. He never named my struggle—he left that up to me. He simply waited on me to respond and open up. My friend understood what I needed better than I did, and God, it seems, was using him to reach me. In sum, I had no chance. So I turned to the group and did something I've never done in front of other men—opened up my heart. And my wall came tumbling down.

The particulars of my struggle aren't important, not important like the way my friends all responded with prayer and empathy that day and how something foundational had changed in me. Before, I was a Christian fighting the good fight. On that day I changed into a Christian who said, "God, I will not fight alone. I will let go of this pride and let my brothers and sisters help me from now on. I will allow my friends to be friends." And that freed me to be a better friend in return.

Don't get me wrong, I wasn't a less authentic friend than the rest to start. I gave everything I had, which perhaps wasn't all that much. Previously I had cut off the essential parts of authentically connecting with others. But now, moving forward, no longer was relating to others going to be a series of steps and counter-steps of conviviality, rather it was to be a symbiotic encounter between hearts and souls. That was shaky ground for me, because it opened me up to being vulnerable.

Transparency always came easily. It was never the problem. I've been known to enjoy a good conversation, been game to exchange ideas about everything that crossed my mind—the latest news, ancient history, atoms and the galaxy, college football, dumb comedies, politics (like I said, dumb comedies), parties, and bad puns. But all that was stiff-arm stuff. Even when I turned to subjects like feelings or the meaning of life it was always done in a detached and observational way. Vulnerability is a whole other dimension. It involves empathy, understanding, feeling, sharing my heart and entering theirs. That's more like an embrace than a stiff-arm, and it was completely foreign terrain to me, perhaps to most guys.

Once I opened up that day with all the guys, my reshaping steamrolled, and I came to understand for the first time my true connection with the body of Christ. Jesus calls me friend, and these men did too.

The biblical word for love between friends is "*phileo*" (Greek). Having Jesus as a friend teaches mutually beneficial thinking, as in, "What is best for you?" and, "What can I do to make your life better and a priority focus of mine?" Friendship in Christ is fellowship, banding together and supporting one another. Today, without it, I'd be miserably lonely, and a big part of me would still be in hiding. Without friends, I would never be as safe, never be as sharp, never be as wise. Accumulated wisdom is always better than the straight-line variety. With authentic friendship, I don't need to have all the answers. There's a whole band of us, and if I don't have the answer, someone near and dear likely does.

There's an illustration I like to use to point out the folly of going it alone, and how, by ourselves, even when we think we see our path clearly, we are often confused. I hold my hand up at arm's length, palm facing me, and say to a friend, "There are certain things about me that I know, but that you only know if I tell you." Then I move my hand, palm still facing inward, but now just a fuzzy mass one inch from my face. "And there are other things about me which I don't know because I'm too close to see them clearly. I can only know those if I show them to you." Finally, I turn my hand around to face him. "Now you can help me."

I've come a long way. I need friends now and I revel in being one in return. I count on them—as they do on me—and it's a relief to know they're there. I also have miles to go. Worn tracks of self-ishness still distract me from asking favors when I should. It's not a worry that they may ask for one in return; that's the easy part. It's the vulnerability, admitting the need to be comforted or helped in some way. That's hard for us tough guys.

Chapter 21

Surviving the Wild Seas

Act like men.

1 Corinthians 16:13

They are appalling and fascinating, these survival-at-sea stories where one speck of a man clinging to what's left of his raft battles sharks, storms, and foaming, devouring seas, and survives. He is tested to the limit. It's a horrible test, but he finds some part of himself he didn't know for sure he had. Whenever I hear these stories, I wonder what I would do.

I'm in the process of finding out.

Every man of God will have a test—maybe not as dramatic as this one, but every bit as epic—a time to face the foaming beast of the world and battle it out. It begins when we accept Christ, is played out mostly in the seemingly mundane, and always it lasts a lifetime.

I know one thing. I do not have what it takes. I have not-to-be-underestimated fleshly instincts. Running from trouble is one. Avoiding pain to heart, loin, and pride are among the others. And now I know why. I have spent my whole life chasing an illusion of what it is to be a man, fearing all the while I'd be exposed as a lesser one.

When I accepted Christ, I carried a lot of false beliefs with me about who I was and what I was made of. I've been throwing those overboard as fast as I can ever since. Wish I knew then what I know now—that I'm a male by birth and a man by choice.

A working definition of manhood: John Wayne, strong man of action and hero of few words. Now that we've gotten that subject out of the way, if you are like me, it has proven a depressing start to a chapter. I compare to John Wayne about as much as a milk-spoiled kitten does to a Bengal tiger. For I have not been manly, not as I would like; certainly not compared to the ideal of legendary actor John Wayne, of whom I am an unabashed fan (though not in my mother's league; that's not possible). Which is why it pains me to concede that he was never the ideal conception of a man anyway. That title belongs to a carpenter from Galilee, Who is seldom held up as the paragon of perfect manhood anymore. Instead, society points increasingly to its own daft versions, most notably that the ideal man would think and act much like a woman—you know, the sensitive man, the nurturing man, the house husband. For which I issue the following politically incorrect alert: That's a bunch of hooey, pilgrim!

In a society long, long ago, I was taught that boys are snips and snails and puppy dog tails, and girls are sugar and spice and everything nice. I believed it then, back when I was blessedly wide-eyed and gullible; still do now, now that I'm squinty-eyed and analytical. Especially since I've learned that God says it's true, just in different words. Read the Bible from Genesis through Revelation and see for yourself. Or for quicker results, give your young kids a Barbie doll and observe: The boys like to throw it against the wall to make its head fall off. The girls like to dress it up and have a tea party (Should've given the boy a toy castle or some plastic army men so he could have some real fun).

The reality is the sexes are wonderfully different. That's how God made us to be. And that's why I will never know what it is to be a woman. Don't want to. I am a man and I am weak. At least I hope to be.

Karate lessons take a man so far, but won't ever cover up his feeling of inferiority among other men. He mistakenly believes courage and toughness relate to how many other men he can beat up.[28] How many karate lessons did Jesus take? None to my knowledge, and no one doubts He's as tough as a whip of cords. So how many karate belts do I need before I'm tough enough? None! That's good, because I have none. There's nothing wrong with karate, dirt under the nails, the gun range, or any other manly pursuits. We're snips and snails after all. But the fact remains that the toughest guy in the room isn't the one with the most brawn, it's the one who loves so much that he would lay down his life for his friends (John 15:13).

Deep down we all know therein lies true strength, that the ultimate essence of manhood is found in sacrifice, and that there is strength in weakness: "That is why, for Christ's sake, I delight in weaknesses, in insults, in hardships, in persecutions, in difficulties. For when I am weak, then I am strong" (2 Corinthians 12:10 (NIV). And if that is the litmus, there's a lot of faux manliness swaggering about.

When I was a kid in grade school, sitting in class fighting boredom, I used to see how long I could hold my breath. My benchmark was a minute, which meant the free dive world record was never in jeopardy, but that mattered to me not. I did it purely as a test of manhood—a rite of passage. I still do things like that, only now my wife has to endure my feats of bravado (She's not much impressed; she's seen me with a head cold). "Watch this, Hun! Watch how many times I can skip this rock. Shoot! Let me try again, that wasn't a good one." Until finally, "These are bad rocks!"

What can I say? Those are the kinds of things men do. It's part of our manhood training for Christ. And this is what I've learned so far in mine:

Men are made to be peaceful warriors. "Let your gentle spirit be known to all men. The Lord is near" (Philippians 4:5).

The tough, brave military man who offers up his life to protect ours, and with equal zeal sweeps his five-year-old girl into his arms, hands her a stuffed teddy bear, and coos, "I love you, sweetie," is the most masculine thing going (I'm not telling him otherwise!). Nevertheless, we don't have to be in the military to be warriors. Being a peaceful warrior is all about the heart—power under restraint, focused on right and good. And that doesn't mean being a pacifist either. Appearances to the contrary, the foaming beast is very real. He prowls around like a roaring lion seeking to devour us all (1 Pet 5:8). For the believer in this world, pacifism is not an option.

Make no mistake, we are warriors fighting for the kingdom of God. And though our tools are unconventional to many—love is the strongest in our arsenal, and turning the other cheek is not weakness, but the ultimate courage—because of who we are in Christ, when the cause is just and our faith and freedom are on the line, we will fight against evil with everything we've got.

Men are made to walk in humility. "God opposes the proud, but gives grace to the humble" (James 4:6, ESV).

These days, the realm of sports is both a positive and a poor reflection on who we've become as a society. Watching pro football as a kid, I recall how typically after a touchdown the player would toss the ball to the referee and jog to the sidelines where his teammates who would shake his hand and pat him on the back. Then he'd go sit down. Low-key elegance. Five decades later and, although there are admirable exceptions, nowadays scoring touchdowns means strutting, beating one's chest, and proclaiming, "I am the man!"

Did I miss something? You scored a touchdown. You didn't pull women and children out of a river flood! But try explaining to such showboats that humility is a virtue, and you're liable to hear, "It ain't braggin' if you can back it up." Such self-centered drivel that deliberately ignores the God-given dignity of the human soul. We have indeed lost our way. I look forward to a day when the interviewer holding the microphone responds: "It most certainly is 'braggin' even if you *can* back it up. If you can't, it's just called lying!" Logic, fellas; humility and logic.

As a child, I was in awe of the heroic men of the Apollo moon missions. Most of the astronauts were confident, humble men (who looked, by the way, like they should be adding up columns of numbers at a metal desk in an accounting office). "Men just doing our jobs," they would have said—which so happened to be hurtling through space in a sealed capsule, risking life and limb to explore the universe, and hoping to return in one piece to planet Earth. I don't recall a single astronaut emerging from his craft mouthing the words, "I am the man," ironically proving what we could see all along—that he really was.

But that's enough about them. Let's talk about me for a little while.

Men are made to persevere. "Let perseverance finish its work so that you may be mature and complete, not lacking anything" (James 1:4, NIV).

Lack of humility and accuracy in writing demand that I tell you that I was a good baseball player in my day, which is to say from ages six to ten. Early on in my career, toward the end of one season I had yet to strike out. Back then, my dad was studying in the evenings at law school and this was the one game he could make that year. I wanted to impress him more than anything. Swing and a miss! Swing and a miss! Swing and a miss! I was crushed, though I kept that to myself for years.

In the meantime, the desire for my father's approval over a simple kids' game left me discouraged enough that I carried the wound of not coming through for my dad for decades, wearing it like a badge of pain, or more like a brand called "fear of failure." That is until God showed me the error of petting my bitterness and I turned to face the foaming beast. Predictably it fled.

All men have setbacks, scars, even defeats. But we're made to get back up. There's a war to win.

Men are made to do purposeful work. "For we are His workmanship, created in Christ Jesus for good works, which God prepared beforehand so that we would walk in them" (Ephesians 2:10).

While we are here in this fallen place, our purpose is to reach others for Christ, bring glory to God, and fulfill the stewardship responsibility of subduing the earth.[29] Pursue any other agenda and the soul will shrivel. It's a pitiful thing.

Long after college and years into business, I had become adequate at climbing the ladder of success, capable in most materialistic pursuits, and a champion at denying that I was wilting. I had no clear purpose, only a habit of measuring up to the agendas of others. Even after coming to Christ, for years I resisted when I heard the call to full-time ministry because I knew that meant forgoing the approvals and yardsticks in business. I had grown accustomed to living for both and craving for more. Since the Tower of Babel, men haven't stopped the vanity of climbing towers of their own making. But scratch the surface of any godless endeavor and you only find futility.

My earthly achievements don't compare, but these three men would tell you the same:

I heard in a sermon once that John D. Rockefeller, one of the richest men in the oil business, was asked toward the end of his life what he had learned that he would tell his younger self. He replied, "I wish I knew when you get to the top of the ladder there is nothing there." Entrepreneur-billionaire Ted Turner was asked, shortly after his company was bought by Time Warner, if he had any regrets. "The only one I can think of is that I didn't get a chance to know what it was like to be really powerful," was his sad reply. And Lee Iacocca, former businessman icon of Chrysler Corporation fame, once said, "Here I am in the twilight years of my life still wondering what it's all about…I can tell you this, fame and fortune is for the birds."

Devoid of purpose, full of self, thoroughly confused. "The slings and arrows of outrageous fortune," as Shakespeare called it.[30] That was those men. That was Solomon for a time. And that is us too, every businessman, farmer, mechanic, or minister when we go it alone. Meaningful work is good, but work can never be meaningful apart from God.

Men are made to be men above all else. "Act like men" (1 Corinthians 16:13).

Inside I know I'm not the man I've built myself up to be in others' eyes. God knows too. I'm more like little Junior hiding a stolen treat behind my back, aware I'm about to have to show my hands anyway. Fine by Junior, because I know Whose I am, and I assent to the process and the destiny prepared for me. "'For I know the plans I have for you,' declares the LORD, 'plans to prosper you and not to harm you, plans to give you hope and a future'" (Jeremiah 29:11, NIV).

And with that eternal view in mind, it occurs to me that a better way to look at the plans God has for me is not as things I have to do, but as inborn parts of my spiritual makeup that I get to do. By God's power within me, I get to live them out.

I get to love and serve my God on the front lines of this spiritual warfare about us, praying with vigilance and vying for every human soul.

I get to keep my eyes on the truth the Bible says about men, not what society is peddling as they clench their fists at my God.

I get to cherish all women and to be a husband of one, with the responsibility to love her and sacrifice irrespective of the consequences or approval if it means protecting her. That means I get to hold the compact umbrella over her head while I get wet. Do I really want it another way?

I get to be a great father—and I hope I was at least a good one. It includes taking my son to the hardware store just to look at tools, and giving my daughters my approval more than my advice. But, foremost, the role ordains that I get to introduce them to Jesus.

I get to respect all men and to have authentic brotherhood in the body of Christ; to bond with them as men in numbers strong who learn together to dig deep in our souls and be who God calls us to be; to know when to step up or fall on our swords; and any other metaphors that are proven to rouse men's souls to work together in full service for our Creator. "A cord of three strands is not quickly torn apart" (Ecclesiastes 4:12).

Mostly, I get to look weak in the eyes of the world so I can be strong for God.

And if none of those "get to's" are enough to inspire a Christian man's soul, there's another one that always does:

"Finally, be strong in the Lord and in the strength of His might. Put on the full armor of God, so that you will be able to stand firm against the schemes of the devil. For our struggle is not against flesh and blood, but against the rulers, against the powers, against the world forces of this darkness, against the spiritual forces of wickedness in the heavenly places. Therefore, take up the full armor of God, so that you will be able to resist in the evil day, and having done everything, to stand firm. Stand firm therefore, HAVING GIRDED YOUR LOINS WITH TRUTH, and HAVING PUT ON THE BREASTPLATE OF RIGHTEOUSNESS, and having shod YOUR FEET WITH THE PREPARATION OF THE GOSPEL OF PEACE; in addition to all, taking up the shield of faith with which you will be able to extinguish all the flaming arrows of the evil one. And take THE HELMET OF SALVATION, and the sword of the Spirit, which is the word of God" (Ephesians 6:10).

Manly stuff.

And the karate belts of the inferiority complex are nowhere to be seen.

Part Five

INTO THE QUIET

Chapter 22

PRAYER REPOSE

*God has instituted prayer so as to
confer upon his creatures
the dignity of being causes.*

BLAISE PASCAL

I went to work with no sense that anything extraordinary was going to happen on that beautiful day. I was looking forward to the lunch I had scheduled with Hal, the eighty-four year-old father of a close friend. I love the elderly and respect their values and experiences, and so was delighted to connect. But more importantly, I'd been meeting with him every few months for some time in the hope of encouraging him to see his need for Christ. Encouragingly to me, he was always interested in hearing more. At lunch, we talked about our families and life in general, and here and there

I found my spots to interject some key points of the gospel. Like always, the lunch ended too soon.

As we headed across the parking lot, I remember thinking, "Oh well, doesn't look like today is the day."

We said our goodbyes, and as I was walking away, Hal called out in an anguished tone, "Why is it so hard to accept Him? I mean, maybe I'm just too selfish" (My soul! It is a rousing nail-biter to see the human will coming to the precipice of surrender).

I tried my dithering best to point the way. "Hal, you know you can go home right now and pray to accept Christ, and on this very day it will be a done deal." He looked to the sky, then to the ground—weighing his options, it seemed. After a few moments I picked up again. "Or you can go over there to your car and sit inside and pray." Then finally, I got out what I really wanted to say: "Or you can pray right here, right now, with me."

I'll never forget that moment. I felt what I can only describe as the white-light presence of the Holy Spirit surrounding us both and encouraging us forward.[31]

"Hal, why don't you go ahead and pray? You know what you're praying for."

He was so close to making his life changing—make that life-receiving—decision that he even simulated a step forward, but just as quickly pulled his foot back from a boundary line only he could see.

"You can do it, Hal. You can—"

He closed his eyes and began to pray, "Jesus, why is it so hard? Show me how to do this. It's just so hard. Amen." Then he paused for a moment, looked right at me, and concluded with, "Well, I guess that's it."

Which were my thoughts too, as in, "That's it, God? But we were so close." My disappointment was interrupted by the next words I heard which turned out to be my own. "Hal, do you want Jesus to be your Savior?"

"Yesss!" (Half pleading.)

"Then ask Him."

Hal, on trembling legs, bowed his head a second time, "Jesus, please come into my life. I know You died for my sins. Please be my Savior, Jesus. Amen." And with that he took a step forward, walked straight across his boundary line, leaned over a truck bed for support, and let out eighty-four years' worth of sighs. Hal was a new man!

"You did it, Hal! God's Spirit lives inside of you now! I'm happy for you, my friend. How do you feel?"

"Relieved!" he answered. And he looked it—for those first moments anyway. Then suddenly his expression changed to one of deep concern, and he said out loud, more to God's ears than to mine, "I think Brenda's saved, but I'm not sure."

I just stood in awe at the miracle of how an eighty-four-year-old man who took a lifetime to receive Christ had now became an inspired evangelist in less than five minutes.

After we agreed to be praying for his wife, we said our real goodbyes—this time as brothers in Christ. As I drove along, I was as emotionally charged as I've ever been. And as I thanked God for the privilege of witnessing what He had just done for my venerable friend, God instantly responded from His heart to mine, as clear as that beautiful day: "As long as you have a breath remaining, never give up hope on anyone, son. Never."

The next morning I sat down to write in my journal and my eyes were drawn to the entry from the day before. I had no recollection of writing those particular words, nor why it was so brief, since ordinarily I write several paragraphs of thoughts and prayers. Here is what it said in its entirety: "Daddy, I know You're going to do great things today. I pray Hal opens his eyes and his heart to You. Guide all I do. In Jesus' name, Amen."

—⁂—

The first prayer I remember hearing was around the supper table at my Uncle Jack's on Easter Sunday. I was a young child who knew nothing of the gospel. But once a year I got to hear his simple, dignified prayers of thanksgiving to God.

Other than that, zippo, nada, not a prayer, until...

I stood with my family on the back porch of my grandparents' home in Miami, Florida, shaken to the core and clinging to a human lifeline of hands, while the local minister guided us in our prayer of grief over the death of my beloved grandmother. She was the spark for us all—our prize—and this was my first experience with death close-up. But somehow, praying to a God that the paternal branch of my family didn't believe existed—me included—felt hypocritical. We weren't the praying types, so exactly what were we doing? Seems we needed Him to exist after all, needed His comfort in our great loss. "Just leave us alone when life is going well, would ya?"

Praying together that day registered to at least one fallow soul as the most comforting and powerful thing he had ever felt. I'm not talking of emotionalism. It was more like raw transcendent presence, which surprised the fool out of me since I wasn't to meet Jesus until two years later.

It was soon after I did meet Him, and early on in my church-going days, that I joined the round-the-clock prayer team, volunteering for the 8:00 PM slot every Wednesday at the church. The first time my turn came around, I walked into a large closet of a room, sat down at a corner desk, opened one of several long gray metal boxes stuffed to overflowing with index cards of prayer requests, and said, "Alrighty, God, do Your stuff." Not fully incompetent, but it was pretty awful. I had no experience, no training, and quickly surmised this was the initiation for both.

Absent a better idea, I pulled out a stout clump of cards and began reading: Darnel lost his job; Francine's mother is in hospice; Jimmy needs a new transmission; and the Jones' daughter needs a new kidney. I felt sorely unqualified and, amidst the dull silence, a bit like a child in time-out. But I also knew I had a job to do, so I began without further delay. And subsequently spent the remaining minutes of my "prayer vigil" in a scatter of mental distraction and random mumblings of self-evaluation, such as, "I don't think I said that right," or, "Say, that was a good one," until finally, "I wonder if there'll be any chicken left over when I get home." And so, slightly less sound of mind than when I began, I left.

I hereby confess, I never went back.

As the years passed, I continued to dip a toe or two in the lukewarm waters of my prayer life and suffered the privilege of other equally woeful experiences. Witness:

I used to memorize an opening prayer in case I was called upon to open for our Sunday school class. I had little confidence I could "conjure up" a prayer on the spot, preferring to perform a prayer rather than risk sharing from my heart. Nothing wrong with memorizing or reading a prayer if it helps one better express his heart. However, here I knew my motive wasn't so much the fear of looking bumblingly dumb to my peers (which ironically is more likely when conjuring a prayer performance), as it was to cover over my fear of letting go and trusting God. I'm sure wanting to appear spiritually mature crept into it as well, which when you get down to it amounts to the same fear of trusting God.

But I am an equal-opportunity conjurer, for I did the same sorts of things even when alone. Not the memorizing part, but the formality of going through a mental check list, meting out of my head instead of letting out of my heart: "God, You're great. I need some things worked out. Help me. Protect them. Comfort, you know, everyone who needs it and stuff. Amen."

Another time I said a prayer for a group of men to open our Bible study: "Lord please bless this food before us..." And He would have been happy to do so had there been any. Not my finest moment!

I could go on. There have been other gaffes and deficiencies of comparable stature up to this very day. This performance nonsense is a persistent nag, and my spotty prayer life is undoubtedly a manifestation of an unripe soul in mid-transformation with far to go. But lest I leave you with the wrong impression, I should add that learning to pray has, at large intervals, been a captivating, numinous journey into the lap of my nurturing Father. Every day now is increasingly that. In fact, I have progressed so rampantly forward that after just twenty short years, I have reached—try not to envy, now—the towering level of "beginner" man of prayer.

I make light of what weighs heavily on many, not for lack of empathy, but because I've come to view prayer as a vital yet liberating matter for any follower of God. It's certainly not a fret-worthy one—not when seen properly against eternity; not when understood as part of a process of this magnificent journey that God's children get to complete to maturity; not when as it turns out, reaching the pinnacle of our prayer-life—intimacy with God—is not impeded by our diverse failures along the way, but mercifully expedited by them.

I don't suppose there is an easier path that would accomplish as much. If there were, we'd be on it.

I see now that I am intended to learn about prayer by this process of triumphs and follies, and mostly the latter. It builds my dependence, which builds my trust, which I do well to place in my Father, whose sustaining love encourages me along. I also see that yet again I have the order all backwards.

Once I thought I was praying to encourage Him to follow me. I've come around—He's rather persuasive. Now when I pray, I follow His lead. Now I see all the prayers as my heart-connection to God and the consummation of my faith. The two go hand-in-hand. When I have the faith of a child, God draws me to Himself. And when I pray, like all good fathers, He sits me in His lap so we can talk. And that's an agreeable place to have a talk, wouldn't you say?

Hard to object to such comforting imagery. So far so good. But now for a claim that is sure to nettle any souls who prefer to "earn their keep" with their Father: I'm always in His lap. Even in my most scoundrelly, inattentive moments, the deepest part of me never stops praying. I hear the gasps, and these would be well-founded if the prayers of my heart originated only from myself. But that's never the case. The Holy Spirit residing in me ensures that even when my soul is not consciously aware of it, nonstop prayers emanate even so. In holy words: "In the same way the Spirit also helps our weakness; for we do not know how to pray as we should, but the Spirit Himself intercedes for us with groanings too deep for words" (Romans 8:26).

I don't stop loving my children when I'm asleep. I don't stop driving when I'm listening to the radio in the car. And I don't stop praying because I'm eating a slice of pizza. By God's grace, it is my nature to pray. His Spirit is in me, and there will always, always be prayers effervescing within.

That is why, seen through the lens of grace, the call to "pray without ceasing" (1 Thessalonians 5:17) is ultimately an encouragement to embrace the natural rhythm and flow of a life of prayer and not a command to get to work.

That is why, as it turns out, I *was* qualified to be on the round-the-clock prayer team, slack as I was.

That is why, even when I pray with a thousand tumbling thoughts racing around my mind, the intent of my heart gets through. So too declares the eloquent prose of Francois Fénelon: "Love, hidden in the depths of the spirit, prays constantly even when your mind needs to attend to something else."[32]

That is why I never say, "No, all's good" when someone asks if there is something they can be praying about for me. Now I say, "Please do."

That is why when I'm asked to pray, or I have the need myself, I pray about every big or little thing. Sometimes right on the spot. Other times on my drive home—eyes wide open, naturally. Sometimes by writing my prayer in a journal, or praying in my Sunday school class, or around the dinner table, or while walking in the woods. Sometimes out loud, or to myself, or in front of others, or in front of the dog (who wonders if I'm on the phone, I think).

That is all gloriously why I have faith in what God is doing—His love, His plan, His wisdom—and not in my jabbering solutions. There are no words I must dispense. There is no need to say or solve diddly. I get to pray. Jesus prays, the Holy Spirit prays, and by God I get to pray!

Kind of takes all the performance out of it, doesn't it?

Prayer is my ongoing conversation with God—I'm never not praying, remember? Though usually it takes turning off the world before I realize it's happening. Those are the moments I am drawn, irresistibly, to engage in the process.

There is a stream within.

The body of Christ around the world prays daily from this stream, sending forth millions of prayers of praise, petition, and gratitude. They are the praying throngs, and where Kingdom matters are concerned they are formidable. Their individual prayers begin as a trickle, then gather and pour into a roaring river. Whenever I stop to truly listen, I'm in awe of the river's power and I'm reminded that I get to be a part of a moving, thriving, multi-million-person prayer team whose prayers stream across God's heart every day. We're talking fearsome power here.

Jesus speaks of the outcome of praying together in the Spirit. "Again I say to you, that if two of you agree on earth about anything that they may ask, it shall be done for them by My Father who is in heaven" (Matthew 18:19). I imagine when a multitude of us agree to pray together, the enemy trembles.

I have witnessed awe-inspiring answers to prayer. Bad habits break, miracles happen, people heal, relationships restore, and broken lives change. I have been a beneficiary of those prayers, and more than likely so have you.

Yet while many of my own prayers have been answered, many of the things I have prayed for didn't come about, not yet or not to my knowledge. And that rankles me, which is one of my newest prayer hurdles, even as I stumble over many of the old ones. Yet with every challenge, the feeling never leaves me that God, above all, desires my trust. Gently, and occasionally vigorously, He encourages me to open up increasingly more about today's events, tomorrow's dreams, any triumphs, and all my hurts—to share my truest heart with Him. That means not mouthing prayers of feigned eloquence or self-seeking solutions, but simply talking with my Father and hearing His heart in return. Most trusting of all, it means to accept His response even when it's "No," or "Wait."

Of course when the answer is "Yes," that brings its own challenge. How I look forward to the day when the urgent requests are answered—the mortgage gets paid, the surgery went well, the life was spared—and I don't forget to thank God, or worse, explain the miracle away as a natural occurrence or one due to extraordinary human effort or skill, forgetting that God working through the circumstance brought forth the result. Again, I have hurdles.

I have seen many prayers answered. I'm also still waiting for answers in vast areas of my life where I have prayed and seen nothing happen. I have no choice but to depend on God then. My faith grows—or does it flow?—the most at those times. It has to. It's not a posture I'm comfortable with. But it is the only satisfying posture. Prayer is not making God a cosmic genie and tossing upwards the baubles of my wants. It is saying, "Father, you give me the desires of my heart from the start, and I shall hold these up to the Holy Wind, and trust You to take it from there."[33] That's it! That's the sweet spot! And when I'm there praying with childlike dependence, God holds me in His arms and smiles.

—⟋⟍—

I'm a grown child now. Today, I'm engaged in full-time vocational ministry, officially sanctioned with God's blessing, you might say, to pray whenever I want, to say grace before meals, to pray over the infirm, to pray for the important and for the ordinary, to—well, to do nothing I couldn't do before when you get right down to it. I just didn't know that early on. But I have acquired one new qualification in all these intervening years since I first mumbled my way through that church prayer closet. I have learned what to pray.

It was about a year after my church vigil, after a hard day at work—one of those days you wonder how you're going to ever be the man God intended, how you're going to provide for your family and live up to their needs and ideals. I kissed my five-year-old son goodnight, turned out the light, and started to walk away when I heard his sweet small voice call to me, "Daddy?"

It was too dark to see his face. "Yeah, son?"

"Daddy, I know the best prayer you can ever say" (out of the mouths of babes).

"What's that, son?" He had my attention.

"I love You, God."

Instant tears began to well. Big ones. "That's beautiful, son. You're exactly right."

"Good night, Daddy," pierced the darkness.

"Good"—I fought to get the words out—"Good night, son. I'm proud of you." By the time I reached the end of the hall I was crying a river, as happy as I've ever been.

That was almost twenty years ago. Prayer remains my lifeline in a tough world, a place already overcome by Jesus, yet where I must wait till He returns. Where every night I pray through its darkness, and my last words are always, "I love You, God."

Chapter 23

QUIETING THE NOISE

*There was a time when silence was normal
and a lot of racket disturbed us.*

HENRI NOUWEN,
WITH OPEN HANDS

I could have been a monk. I'd have been the guy who walks into the monastery and proceeds with few provisions to my spartan room, where first I test the cot (*ee-ee-ee-ee*), then the sink (same squeak the cot made). That's it!—the entire adornments of the room. It's not supposed to be the Hyatt.

Instantly bored, I don my monk's robe and mosey out to the grounds—head down in conspicuous contemplation, of course—then off to the far side of the pond where I settle onto a bench, already occupied by another monk, and which I choose over the nearby empty one in order to demonstrate for this perfectly noiseless human my equal mastery over silence. Five minutes in, I'm splashing handfuls of pebbles in the water, and I turn to him and query: "So, things going pretty good for you so far?" He gets up and walks away. Like I said, I could never have been a monk.

You wouldn't know it by watching me chatter my way through the years, but I've desperately wanted to quiet the noise in my life. But timely silence is tough for me. To be timely silent is to not need to defend myself or make sure they see me in the best light, to let all my striving thoughts be still, and to allow my demanding flesh to be crucified. In just this past week, sentiments of the following kind coursed through my non-monk noggin more than once: "Lord, my head is spinning, my nerves are fraying, I have no idea which is my next best move. There are ceaseless interruptions yelling my name, competing for my thoughts and feelings. Tell me which one is Yours, Lord." I don't think my mania is unusual for mankind in this twenty-first frenzy of ours, though you might disagree and believe me to have a worse condition than is normal. Either way, it's all relative. For most of us, it's raining pebbles on the pond.

In the comparatively still first century AD, "Jesus often withdrew to lonely places and prayed" (Luke 5:16, NIV). How much more, then, do we need to find peace and quiet in these crazy times? I try to make time to do that, aware that it is good for me, and that I will eventually—on one side of Heaven, at least—be a natural at it. So I seek my quiet spaces when and where I can so as to enter a place of peace as much as possible, and subsequently find

I can take the solitude for just so long. Too much of it scares me, evokes feelings I don't like to feel.

Henri Nouwen in *The Way of The Heart* writes, "In solitude I get rid of my scaffolding: no friends to talk with, no telephone calls to make, no meetings to attend, no music to entertain, no books to distract me—naked, vulnerable, weak, sinful, deprived, broken—nothing."[34] Reflexively, I call that loneliness. But that misses the mark. I'm not lonely at those times; I'm alone—with God. That means being vulnerable in plain sight of His transforming intentions. And that is instinctually uncomfortable; at least until I recover my better reasoning and accept that in the quiet He also offers me the wisdom of His counsel and the relief of His healing presence.

So Father, lead me through this quiet and deal my flesh its mortal blow, through the stillness if you must, if that's what it takes for me to learn to thrive in Your peace and to hear You even more. I pray this as I write, not as a brave Christian soldier, but as a nervous one, at least aware that if I enter this place of holy solitude enough times, one day I'll tire of all my noise-making and get from head to heart that the best part of the solitary turn is in the listening.

"Your ears will hear a word behind you, 'This is the way, walk in it,' whenever you turn to the right or to the left," (Isaiah 30:21) is not a bygone pep talk, but the Word of God, and an ongoing prophetic truth. I have experienced it myself many times. I hear God.

"No way! You're trying to tell me you hear God's voice?" I've been asked that in incredulous tones more than once. Perhaps they are mistaking my declaration to mean that God speaks to me at my beck and call and in stereotypical booms which quake the room:

"Good morning, Kevin! Eggs over easy sound good to you to-day, champ? (And the dishes all fall from the cupboards)."

No, never heard that. The voice I hear—when I hear it—is as soft and clear as the rustling leaves of the river birch tree shading my hammock. That same clarity is echoed every time He speaks to me in His myriad creative ways: in my heart where He resides; in my conscience where together we commune; in passages from books to which I'm providentially drawn; in scenes from movies that move my soul; in a talk with a close friend who tells me something I needed to hear. Through all these ways, God's precious voice, in a low whisper, says, "Not that way, my boy. This way."

I wish I heard Him more. On all the little things even: "Your shoes are untied; keep your head down on the follow through; re-member to look 'em in the eye and smile." But I understand I put limitations on what I'll allow myself to hear. My stiff-necked ways and puny faith are barriers I use to censor the miraculous ways He chooses to talk with me. I'm not suggesting I can cause God to speak to me. When I try that, I hear—wait for it—nothing. What I am suggesting is that when I call out to Him in the full dependence of my heart and listen for His voice, when it comes, I hear words and timbres of such staggering beauty and soul-soothing calm that it fairly unstiffens my knees till I succumb to my long-desired re-spite in the hammock of my soul.

And I think now I know how the quiet saints among us do it. More importantly, I think now I know why.

For us habitually restless sorts, it's easy to doubt that we have such a restful place as this deep inside our souls—"an interior castle," as St. Teresa of Avila called it.[35] Nonetheless, we do. In fact, peace is so worthy a gift as to be the third-listed dimension of the fruit of the Spirit within us: love, joy, peace, et cetera. All we need do is abide in Jesus and it is ours.

I forget that often, especially at 3:00 AM when I'm tossing and turning, trying to work out real or imagined problems. If I can't sort them out when I'm awake, what makes me think I'll succeed when I'm half asleep? My best solutions are always the ones God brings to mind in His time, anyway. Fretting in the wee hours usually feels like the world's time, not His. And that thought sparks a revelation that until recently I have overlooked. What I seek far more than to silence the decibels without is to find a peace within: it is not so much a silence of words I desire—though fewer of them would be nice—but a silence of clamoring thoughts. Here's hoping I find that motivated practice defeats years of bad habit soon.

When I was a young child, I was conscripted into an annual forced march through the department stores to buy new clothes for the upcoming school year, whereupon I would unfailingly develop what I termed, "shopping legs"—the commensurate loss of will and able muscle to take a single step more. Usually this was signaled by way of whining about the effects of gravity on small legs and with compound complaints of tedium, swarming shoppers, and missing out on playtime with friends (incidentally, I still get shopping legs today, though curiously never at the hardware store). When inevitably my protests did not lead to an early departure, I would crawl under the long racks of hanging clothes to retreat from my tour of sorrows into a hidden fortress of peace known only to me; that is until my mother would see familiar sneakers connected to skinny legs and pull me out. Hello world!

My how little things have changed! This many years later and the moments of serenity rarely come about easily or naturally for me. More than ever I retreat to my fortress—no, not the clothes rack! Though I'd try it if I could get away with it. Today I have a fortress of a different sort. When the child in me wants to throw a tantrum about the noise of it all, I transcend the disturbance from out of my impenetrable place of peace—God within. I'm not yet consistent at it. Come to think of it, I've never been any place as noisy as my head when I'm trying to be quiet. But I am progressing nicely toward a new habit. "You keep him in perfect peace whose mind is stayed on you," (Isaiah 26:3, ESV). Yes! Please, yes!

And now let me brag plainly. Though I had many failures last week, twice, maybe thrice, I experienced that transcendent feeling of peace where I overcame challenging scenarios of stress. You know the kind—traffic jams, relational tensions, slow-talking Uncle Fred sharing his one travel story again. Once that peace emerged, it was as if a great quiet enveloped me and all the rest faded into a manageable background as the peace of God took center stage. The stress became merely faded distractions, much like the gonging grandfather clock that used to annoy me, but now, years later, I rarely notice at all—it has ebbed away into the peaceful surroundings. Or when I do remember it, it just sits there in the corner all pleasant and chiming on the hour for me.

An abiding sense of peace is the birthright of all believers. It is also the only way to rise above the noise of the world. For too long we have allowed ourselves to be led about by the world's frenzy, habitually ignoring the better option of facing it through the quiet places, without and within, which God provides. When we accept and enter that provision, we accordingly become better equipped to roam this world and take our place in it the way He intended— as better companions to each other and as beacons of light to the lost (Matthew 5:14). Try to venture out beforehand, at our own peril always, and we will get caught up in the wash of the manic pace, and perhaps be too eager to break the silence when sitting on a bench with a monk.

Chapter 24

THE SIMPLE LIFE

Simplicity is the ultimate sophistication.

LEONARDO DI VINCI

One hour turned into half a day as I tried to reorder my Granddad's shed. I meant well. Courtesy of Hurricane Andrew the previous year, the shed had shifted maybe six inches so that it no longer lined up with the ramp, thus making it a tighter squeeze for the riding mower. The project seemed simple enough, quite manageable really—move all the stuff out, then using the end of a long crowbar, scooch the shed back into place. Estimated time: about sixty minutes.

And with that ill-fated estimate in mind, I began moving the items—the mower, rakes, shovels, wires, cords, tools, coffee tins of nails and screws, rusty paint cans, boxes upon boxes of metal parts to once-useful things, and other obscure such and such the likes of which you've never seen other than perhaps in your own shed—out to the yard. Nearly three hours later the shed was empty, and I attempted said scooching, and nothing happened. Turns out the shed far outweighed its contents.

Posthaste, I reversed my process, estimating—correctly this time—that in minutes Granddad would saunter out and see this mess. As I worked in a purposeful dither, I soon discovered that I would have had an easier time doing a jigsaw puzzle with all the pieces turned backwards, which is coincidentally how the innards of the shed ended up, and which is why, upon his arrival, Granddad gave forth a genial but nonetheless disappointed sigh followed by a three-beat "*mmgh, mmgh, mmgh!*"—emphasis on the last—which translated means, "Thanks for nothing, number four grandson." This right before he informed me that previously it had been no real bother getting the mower in and out, and if it ever became one he would simply expand the ramp with a few bags of concrete.

Simple solution. And I missed it, thus making my day, and his future search for a socket wrench, more difficult than they needed to be. All was not lost. I still got to eat his signature spaghetti for dinner.

Love God. Love others. (Eat Granddad's spaghetti.) Pretty simple. But I make life so much more complicated. I have hungered for simplicity all my livelong days but only recently did I come to realize what I really seek is the contentment behind it. I know I have everything I need to be content: "Blessed be the God and Father of our Lord Jesus Christ, who has blessed us with every spiritual blessing in the heavenly places in Christ" (Ephesians 1:3). But apparently I'm not sure how to live with that. So I spend my time trying to make all the ramps line up. It is one of my chief vanities, born of deep character flaws and built upon generations of envy-prone earthlings. That is to say, I come by it honestly.

And remorseless Madison Avenue stokes it all with lies.

Although I'm an unabashed free market proponent who believes in hard work, finding satisfaction in a job well done, and enjoying the fruit of one's labor, the world (read that: Satan and his minions) has a different agenda. It depends on persuading us that we are never satisfied—that we need always more, more, more—and it thrives on that discontentment. I, for one, am susceptible to its tactics. The examples of my vulnerabilities are too numerous to name, so I will target the grandest one that applies to us all, the one we fill with all the other belongings we "must" have: the home.

Consider that today in America, a typical middle-class family lives in a home far superior in comfort to that of the wealthiest classes from two-hundred years ago. Yet we take for granted the electricity that allows us to see at night and run all our stuff, climate control to dial in perfect temperatures, and not to mention, indoor-outdoor plumbing, water heaters, and microwaves. Oh my! What's more, the average home size has grown from 1,600 to 2,600 square feet of living space in a little over four decades.[36] Nevertheless, if the McFeebies down the street have a new game room addition, I'm suddenly uncomfortably claustrophobic. I have noticed that such discontented thoughts are never accompanied by a sober evaluation of whether my house suits me in and of itself, and certainly not by how much better I have it than my ancestors. That's why I think things like, "Golly Gee!"—that's the edited version—"I wish I had a really nice workshop like Lenny Frankfurter does."

I look to others to determine my level of contentment and end up predictably grumbly. Meanwhile, my gratefulness to God for the blessings He's already bestowed gets lost in the complications of my own making. I certainly can't blame today's culture. If I lived "back when"—in so-called simpler times—I'd have the same vice:

Me: I wish I had ten-spoke wagon wheels like Farmer Dibbs's instead of these spindly six-spoke ones.

Sears, Roebuck Catalog: Happy to oblige!

Progress is good, but discontentment—well, sadly discontentment has always filled the voids in ungrateful human souls. Which embarrasses me to no end. I understand why someone who has rejected God would be discontented, but I have no such excuse.

When I consider the lifestyle of anyone who owns a sprawling mansion today, why do I feel instantly discontented? I already have way more than I deserve: my favorite chair, a warm, soft bed, high-definition television, a kitchen filled with special ovens, which are in turn filled with assorted treats I skillfully hunted down at the corner grocery—amidst an intimidating sea of foodstuffs and a horde of hungry competitors, I might add—where, through it all, I survived by wits untold and returned home with whatever I wanted (My wife, incidentally, wasn't sure why I was so proud, and wondered why the trip took two hours).

Safely back at home, I even have an outdoor grill for those times when I want a rather quaint way to gather around to visit with family and friends. I also have my own yard. Not the Biltmore Gardens, but a quasi-manicured lawn just the same. On occasion I find a nice, soft spot to lie down on the freshly-mowed lawn, fully reposed with a stalk of grass between my teeth, a glass of lemonade by my side. Or is that in my imagination? Either way, it doesn't happen enough. In my heart and mind I want simplicity, but instead I spend most of my energy gathering goods and chattels which become possessions that keep getting in my own cluttery way.

Comedian George Carlin used to do a bit where he talked of a trip to Hawaii where he took along what he thought was his important stuff, all in luggage filled to the brim. Till he needed to leave his hotel for a day to go to a nearby island, and so packed an even smaller bag for that trip. This, he deduced, was his *really* important stuff. That is, until he went on a day hike from there and packed a smaller bag still in which he could carry his really, really important stuff. Really.

I long for a simpler life. Have I said that? It bears repeating.

John Muir, the nineteenth-century naturalist, knew about simplicity, and he lived it for years. A remarkable lifestyle choice by a man (perhaps a believer, perhaps not) who had every opportunity to cash in on the lifestyle of his wealthier famous friends, but for years preferred instead to dwell in his small cabin along Yosemite Creek in the middle of his beloved Sierra Mountains. Imagine the advantage of preferring a small house, of not needing to move every three years to accrete yet another room. Imagine, if you dare, the liberation of going through life content with the lesser option. Lesser in the world's eyes that is.

Years ago we took a family vacation to break up the rut of routine and rented a John Muir-ish cabin in the beautiful mountains of the West. In the early evenings, after each long, pleasant day of hiking, we'd sit under a shade tree with the kids. No television. No cell phones or computers. Just each other, hanging out together, everyone so relaxed and drawing close again. Two weeks later we returned home, and within twenty-four hours we were all sequestered in our separate corners in front of our electronic gadgetry. We had shade trees in our yard, but we didn't sit under them.

—❦—

"But seek first His kingdom and His righteousness, and all these things [food, drink, and clothes], will be given to you as well" (Matthew 6:30). That's as simple as it gets. And when I pray with that priority, God reminds me that simplicity is mine for the choosing, same as it always has been. I don't have to travel to the agreed-upon amazing places, be seen at the best parties, or check off some imagined list of great experiences. I have the love and approval of my Father now and always, and He will forever be my greatest experience. He alone offers a life of nonpareil contentment. And if that's what lies behind the simple life, what more do I need? Easy answer: nothing. But as I say, I do complicate things.

The simple life is the better life, unquestionably. I like my new truck with the gizmos, but I miss my old one with the bench seat more. No frills, and it felt right. But that's not the half of it. I miss my red bike from childhood. I miss walking to school, and skipping rocks across streams. Mostly, I miss being able to relax. I don't sleep as well under my store-bought comforter. I slept better under the old hand-stitched quilt, made with love and care. To this day, my all-time favorite gifts on birthdays or at Christmastime are not expensive or flashy, they are the handmade ones. A bookmark is a heavenly gem when it is decorated with a sparkly unicorn and words by your child. Which reminds me of the saying, "When the house is burning who grabs the TV?" What is wrong with us?

I know what's wrong with me. I became an adult so-called and now too often spend time absorbed in accumulations and not God. I first entered this mouse maze because I was told by many that it was the better way through life, even though I knew better. Why the diatribe now? Oh, I don't know. The culmination of disappointment with myself, I suppose. Certainly with the gimme-gimme world we live in—that we must endure. And frustration with my failure to get out of the maze, or more like off this monkey wheel (and I don't even know what that is, but it's right). And sadness that my exhausted constitution forgets how to relax and rest and simplify.

Many give up, declaring it to be impossible to achieve such stillness of soul in a society of motion. However, the stillness I desire has little to do with motion, but instead with faithfully abiding in Jesus. That's why I know it's attainable, though I admit it's a challenging state of maturity to reach for, and I will assuredly run out of years before God is through with me on that one. To assuage my guilt, I tell myself the stuff isn't the problem, the love of it is, whereupon at once I respectfully disagree with my own rationalization. It is both.

My shed is full. My closets are full. My schedule is overflowing. Yet I keep cramming more into my life, most emblematic of which are these timesaving devices that never bring about the promised saner pace. Instead, they pack more things between what free moments I had left, till I have no time to spend with friends who happen to drop by. Though of course they never do anymore because they're busy that day putting more things in their rented storage sheds. I should know. That's why I don't go to their houses either. It's exasperating, yes? Once you're in the maze of excess, it's hard to get out. Or is it?

It's not as if I don't have a role model to follow.

Jesus lived a simple life. He rode a donkey and wrote with His finger in the dirt. Now we fly across the continents in jet planes typing on computers in our laps. Had the Son of God been chosen to be born into our times, I don't know if He would have flown in planes, but it doesn't seem like it. Or if He did, He wouldn't be clutching a laptop. He'd be talking with His neighbor, or His

Father. The record is clear: Jesus went about His Father's business, always contentedly, and with minimal stuff.

Meanwhile, here I sit tethered to a houseful of collected wants, even as I aspire to live out what I already know: Jesus is all I need. "More than that, I count all things to be loss in view of the surpassing value of knowing Christ Jesus my Lord, for whom I have suffered the loss of all things, and count them but rubbish so that I may gain Christ" (Philippians 3:8). What a glorious hope! To fill my heart and not my clinging hands. I know this much: the day I walk in single-minded devotion to Christ over the world is the day I finally find the contentment I've been seeking. I hope today's that day. You listening, Madison Avenue? I am not working for you anymore!

Nor, I must remember, am I working for Jesus (Acts 17:25). I don't work for this life He's given me; I walk contentedly in it. That's the goal. And surprisingly, I'm finding that that liberating process is less about casting off the clutter and more about taking the time to do what I was placed here to do: Love Him, love others, point the way—in my own way—to Him. The beauty is that He gives me enough time to do that without the need for my frantic pace. As one preacher aptly put it, "If I run out of time at the end of the day to accomplish my to-do list, I've taken on some things God never asked me to do."[37] Oh me of little faith, it's all true.

Knowing this, I have tried to emulate the contented ways of men and women of faith. For an entire week once, I turned over a new leaf. I whittled on a stick on the front porch instead of going to the store to buy another power tool; drove in the slow lane all the way to town and back, without the radio on; intentionally said "no" repeatedly so as to keep my calendar free for whatever—spontaneity, people, rest; and ate several inexpensive meals made from scratch, slowly and leisurely and not on a TV tray.

It was a good week and I enjoyed the whole experience while it lasted. But in the back of my mind (or should I say in the immaturity of my flesh), by weeks-end I felt like I was falling behind some imaginary standard of progress that kept wheedling in my head: "The days are burning past, friend, and you're getting behind. You gotta move faster to keep up."

Keep up? Monkey wheels *and* mouse droppings! Are we to suppose that gentlemen farmers in days of old had no margin in their lives? We know they worked hard, really hard. They had to eat. But do we really think they didn't have time to pet the dog, admire the sky, watch the birds, and thank God for it all? I know this much: they didn't stare at an electronic screen all day and half the night, which is what I'm doing by the way, because it beats writing all this longhand.

Lord help me. That bears repeating too.

—⁂—

My youngest daughter Kymberly loves to travel. She's the adventurer in the family and has seen her share of this world. A while back, after returning from a mission trip to an impoverished village in Africa, she excitedly informed me that they were the happiest people she'd ever met. And that made me sad, because I knew she was right, and it exposed the futility of my own overly complicated life. Then she told me that many of them were Christians, and that made me proud—proud because she had witnessed firsthand, and now understood something vital, that I myself struggle with in the moments of my discontent: these people who slept on dirt floors and walked two hours every morning to fill their buckets with drinking water lived life with a song on their lips and joy in their hearts for good reason.

One blazing afternoon, a woman from the village who had become fast friends with Kymberly was passing by and asked her why she looked so down. When my daughter explained she was just tired, her friend, in lilting accent, said, "Kymberly, then let me pray for you," then she set her water bucket down and knelt on the warm red clay and prayed in unrestrained, spontaneous reliance upon God. Simple solution.

And mine for a price if I want it. Just give up the world, that's all.

Part Six

INTO THE NIGHT

Chapter 25

TRAVELING LIGHT

Thou shalt have no other gods before me.

EXODUS 20:3

Once upon a time there was a burgeoning Christian, full of excitement over his new-found life. He had met his Creator and couldn't have been more encouraged. Everything he could do to further that feeling was his obsession. So he studied his Bible, went to church, prayed often, met with spiritual mentors, read books by the spiritual giants of the faith, and even golfed a bit (just making sure you're paying attention).

You know by now I'm describing my story—one that, in its essence, fits many of us. As for me, I did pick up golf, more or less. At least enough to become decent at it and not just be traipsing through unlit woodlands. In those early years of my faith, my good friend Rob (he who cared enough to put me on the spot in our men's group that fateful day), was my most frequent golfing companion. To offset his many attributes, he had the annoying habit of always being organized, with clothes neatly pressed and all his gear spit and polished just like everything else he did (and that is the worst thing I can say about him, which is also annoying).

In the realm of business, whenever we traveled, my goal was to mimic his movements as we prepared for our various meetings, reasoning that by way of these time-motion imitations, I would be squared away and prepared. Unfortunately, it never worked. Papers were sticking out of my briefcase as I entered most conference rooms, my tie always askew. On the golf course my lack was worse.

On a sunny day of infamy, we were at the first tee preparing to tee off with some friends. After everyone else hit their drives, they looked back to find me stooped over and digging through my very full golf bag for a tee. My car keys were in one hand, a golf ball in the other, my gnarled glove from my last golf outing six months earlier was in a decrepit wad on the ground, one shoe was untied, and my shirt was out in the back—the usual. At that moment, up to both elbows looking for supplies, I overheard one of the foursome say to Rob, "What's up with Kevin? He's always in the bag." A well-aimed observation, and its truth provided paroxysms of great mirth for three out of four of the group for the entire eighteen holes that day.

Later, as I drove home (as I recall I still had my golf glove on), I happened to be reviewing my early journey of faith—how it was often marked by encouraging advances into God's heart, but recently had begun to slow somewhat with the heft of baggage I had collected along the way. And it hit me that the earlier comment, intended as humorous regaling among golfing buddies, was an apt assessment of my character as well.

Well that was once upon a time. It has been two decades since, and now I'd like to share something pithy about my reform. But I can't. To this day, in most matters of my life, I expend great effort sorting through the extraneous in search of life's essentials—I'm often in the bag. Of course when you lug around a passel of idols, it's hard not to be.

I don't need to write out the definition of an idol here to know what it is—my soul lets me know every time one of those panhandling impostors clangs its way in. But to our mutual unease, here's the definition anyway: "a representation or symbol of an object of worship; broadly: a false god" (Merriam-Webster). *Clang!* The way I read it, that means anything extraneous to the journey into the heart of God qualifies. *Clangity clang!*

Jesus, as man, had no idols. Satan tempted Him with the dross of the temporal, but Jesus held fast and didn't allow anything into His heart that wasn't from His Father (Matthew 4:1-11). That's what I aspire to, which is a good choice since that's what God ultimately has in store. But for the time being, back on terra firma where I rove, mentally and emotionally I'm lugging around enough idols that on some level, I must think I need them. They are my security, I reason; my diversions, my comforts. Mislabel them what I will, God has shown me—to my great discomfort—that they are my idols and nothing more.

God gave the commandment, "Thou shalt have no other gods before me" (Exodus 20:3, KJV). And that would put me in poor stead were I under the law, for I have too many to count. However, He is a Father of grace, and I am no longer under the condemnation of the law (long grateful sigh). Even so, I still have a problem: namely, these false gods I haul around are an awful hindrance to the closeness I seek with God, and they are unrelenting little fiends.

That is to say, the idols of my life continue to emerge in such unending forms that I've finally figured rightly that I'll be scrounging through my mess, tossing out idols for the rest of my life. Sure I talk big about wanting to get rid of them—"God I want to be willing. Please make me willing." I even follow that with an earnest promise to blow every one of them to kingdom come. Then I don't do it. It's not for lack of enthusiasm, I can tell you. It's just that the desperation of a New Year's resolution is not the way. There's only one way out of these woods: prayer, trust, and patience for a lifetime, no less. I have to take the long view.

The words from the angel-winged hymn, "Amazing Grace" portray a comforting perspective: "When we've been there ten thousand years...we've no less days to sing God's praise than when we've first begun."[38] My soul longs to be there, free and grateful. However, first I have to get through my present reality, which reminds me that were I to live ten thousand years on this earth, I wouldn't come close to jettisoning all the things I tend to put before God. That's not hyperbole; I have specifics that lead me to think it is so.

Allow me to count the ways. Some of my nearest and dearest idols, in no particular order:

Marriage. I have often left God out of my marriage. I am called to leave and cleave so two can become one (Genesis 2:24), yet it has to be God *and* me, then God *in* me, or there can be no God *and* us. Some people exaggerate about having the "perfect marriage." But to have a perfect marriage without God at the heart is a fanciful impossibility.

Children. I've loved them, raised them, given them everything I knew to give. And at times I've tried to claim them and take credit for their accomplishments even though God only asked that I steward them and give them back to Him.

Ministry, or any other work. There is good work to be done, yet it's so easy to wrap my identity around my work and to forget that my effort apart from God's will is not good work and will not survive eternity. I think much of what I've done to date won't make it, and I hope to change that forthwith.

Money. That persnickety idol! When I have plenty of resources, I still worry. And when I don't have plenty, I think about it too much instead of trusting God with my money—I mean His money. Every time I read the Parable of the Talents (Matthew 25:14-30), I'm jolted to the core.

<u>Home</u>. It's *my* castle, right? Wrong! I correct myself. I'm a caretaker, grateful for the blessing of the home He provides.

Those were the easy ones! When I dig deeper I begin to see more subtle idols:

<u>Approval seeking, or its flip side, the fear of rejection</u>. Affirmation is good, but not when I make an idol of what people say or think about me, wanting to be affirmed by my peers more than my desire for God to get all the glory. "The fear of man brings a snare" (Prov 29:25).

<u>Sex</u>. Okay that one's not subtle. I'm going to move along now, thank you.

<u>Nature</u>. I'm no pantheist; I realize that nature is not God. But I enjoy it in all its variety to such a degree that sometimes I forget to behold the Creator more than the creation.

And how about these three doozies?

<u>Health, Happiness, and Comfort</u>. If these can become idols, any-thing can! They're good desires when they're genuine desires of the heart—my ever-loving Father wants these things for me too after all—but treacherous when I require it of Him or put these circum-stances above Him. "For My thoughts are not your thoughts, Nor are your ways My ways," (Isaiah 55:8) says the God Who guides

the stars and tides, and holds life and death in His hands. He has His reasons and I can't make it a requirement that He make my life one of ease. Ask Job.

The list goes on and on. As far as I can tell, the corpus of my offenses has no limit. I have idols of friendship, of time, of sports... oh, never mind; it is too depressing to recount. Let me just say that all my idols have one thing in common—they take a beautiful gift from God and twist it into something that can be misused by the most conspicuous false god of them all: Self. You know, Me. Mine. This. That. Mine. Me. *CLANG!* It's got a catchy beat, but I can't live to it.

Nor will my me-first treasures survive it. All the things I exploit to fill the cravings of my flesh are doomed to stay behind "where moth and rust destroy," (Matthew 6:19) which is the deserved fate for all idols, and some would say for my golf clubs, though for a different reason.

In all, trying to coax my satisfaction from the good things God created instead of God Himself leaves me feeling empty every time. It's a glorious thing to worship the true King. Nothing else compares. No wonder beneath the facade of my temporal deities lives a soul wanting, aware that only God on high can make it dance. Aware, too, that His triumphant plan ensures I won't be bringing any idolatrous baggage into Heaven with me, only my dancing shoes. And for that great hope, I accept how He chooses to shape me for that eternity. Lord knows I'm not qualified to do the shaping. I am qualified, however, to let go of my proud control and allow Him to lead me, one discarded idol at a time, to the destiny He has planned.

So what am I waiting for? At this point, awareness—that light-bulb moment, so I can identify with clarity the next idol to throw on the burn-pile. I know that sounds like idealistic overstatement. I've said "good riddance" before and then backed away, and here I go promising yet again. But I find great solace that in those times when I've made cast-off pronouncements with my heart—and not just screeched and hollered with my lips—another impostor soon hit the heap.

A wise apostle proclaimed, "You have been set free from sin" (Romans 6:18, NIV). This I claim now, with all my heart: "I am free from sin! This bondage will vanish!" Thus I know there's another expulsion coming soon.

Nobody said it would be easy, but a resolute God, for my own good, has me in the middle of an ongoing process of letting go of all the idols of my flesh, and repositioning every person, place, and thing I try to put ahead of Him. And there is no end in sight. Why should there be?

After Jesus was tempted by Satan in the wilderness, "Then Jesus said to him, 'Go, Satan! For it is written, "YOU SHALL WORSHIP THE LORD YOUR GOD, AND SERVE HIM ONLY."' Then the devil left Him; and behold, angels came and began to minister to Him" (Matthew 4:10-11).

I believe God's angels are waiting to do the same to me. They are blessedly patient beings from where I stand, considering how my soul is taking its sweet time rebuffing the enemy. It hasn't helped that I spent so many years trying to overcome the temptations of my idols on my own. Praise God that sometime ago, after countless failed attempts, I finally took hold of an untried thought: I'm not expected to do this by my own efforts; I'm to let God handle it for me.

That's why these days I simply pray, "Lord, show me the way to the center of Your heart, where You allow no idols to dwell." Then I watch God smash to smithereens the latest idol He has in His kindness shown to me. Soon enough the next one is revealed, and we do it all again. For God wants what is best for me even more than I do. That's why I learned several idols ago to no longer say, "Well that seems to be all the big ones; I wonder what He has left?"

Chapter 26

MOVING ON

Many think that dying to themselves is
what causes them so much pain.
But it is actually the part of them that still
lives that causes them the problem.

FRANCOIS FÉNELON

When I think of how fast my children have grown up, it upsets me. So I try not to think about it. But that never works. Has it really been thirty years? I was just watching my wife getting her epidural. "Yes, Honey, I'm fine. The important thing is how are you?" said I, nobly, and prior to the now oft-told fainting-yet-still-walking-while-simultaneously-groping-for-a-nearby-bed-and-hoping-it-wasn't-occupied episode. At least mom and baby were fine (see there—noble). It seems a week ago that I was taking my youngest to his soccer game. I was the coach. That is meritoriously laughable, believe me. Ruefully laughable is the fact that it wasn't last week, it was almost twenty years ago!

A few years later, on our family vacation, we drove around Yellowstone National Park and played the "Animal Game." I can still picture most of the animals. I won by the way. As the driver I naturally saw the sundry creatures first, thus racking up big points, which is the reason I chose the game.[39] That and keeping the children cheerfully occupied. As I drove along espying wildlife, I remember contemplating the thought that before too long all four of them would be teenagers at the same time, and their freewheeling childhoods would be over. Today, of course, none of them are teenagers. There's mercy in that, but I'd do it again.

Good memories. Good times. I cherish those times. And in case you haven't noticed, I struggle to surrender them. To surrender anything, in fact.

If I have a worse condition than squeezing the fool out of the idols of my past, having unsurrendered flesh is a good candidate. Of course, the two conditions are related. The idol is the problem; surrender is the solution. But how in the world do I surrender with open hands when I'm afraid to let go and move on? I hold on for too long and I know I'm dead wrong to do it. At least I can take solace in the fact that my heart accepts the challenge of letting go. Gotta let the winds keep taking you; can't hold on to this ledge forever, lad. It's not that I'm the adventurous type, just more afraid of staying than leaving.

As I reflect back over the years, I don't believe there are neat, tidy stages of life, not in any true sense. There is, rather, one continuously flowing stream of air that takes us away, as we choose which outcroppings to reach for to catch our breath and avoid surrender.

—⁂—

When I was a kid wrestling with my buddies in the front yard, one of the favorite moves of every boy was to get the other guy in a classic behind-the-back armlock. You've probably done it. You clasp his wrist tight and pull up a little at a time while simultaneously commanding, "Say 'Uncle!'" The other guy (your best friend usually), after much writhing and pleading, ultimately concludes by shrieking, "Uncle!" At that point, you had to stop. It was a rule, universally understood by boys everywhere. Once he gives in unqualifiedly, there is no warrant to continue. Many times I was on the receiving end of such exquisite fun, and looking back now I realize it never once crossed my mind *not* to say, "Uncle!" Perhaps because it was only a silly kid's game and not worth the pain of resisting. Perhaps because it was a portent of the necessary surrender of my soul.

Today, much older (and with arthritis in one elbow for some reason), I see how God uses the pain of my struggles to help me recognize my need to surrender everything to Him. Charles Solomon in his book, *The Rejection Syndrome*, observed, "Many want the peace, joy, and power of resurrection life, but few desire the death of the Cross which is the precursor to that life. The Cross was never popular and never will be. Self-effort is appealing and many Christians will work themselves to death to keep from dying!"[40] Some, it seems, won't ever say, "Uncle!"

I've certainly known people who won't give up the fight for their eternal soul no matter what. Even if they could be convinced there is an all-powerful God Who loves them and offers to take care of them, they'd still rather make their own choices and live by their own rules. That's the opposite of surrender. It's called willfulness. Warn them that if they continue down this road it will damn their souls, and nothing comes back but sneers and blank stares. I've tried talking with some of these people for years, walked through big stretches of life with them, and seen them age. Now it's half past damnation and still they don't care. Feigned nonchalance? It doesn't seem like it. There's no need to feign if you really don't care. These people aren't acting. "God, You're not there, but if You are, You'll be kind enough to leave me be." I warned you about my being presumptuous. I realize I can't know for sure where they stand with Him, but it is beyond sad to me that they outwardly dismiss Him with a shrug.

To the best of my recollection, that was never me. I always wanted there to be a God. Even before I knew Him, I needed Him to exist. I sought Him through every step of my rebellion. That makes perfect sense to me now because I've learned that He was calling me forth all along. What continues to baffle, however, is how my issues with fleshly rebellion have persisted long after I became a follower of Jesus. As I inched ahead in my spiritual growth, I could see all the ugly thoughts and behaviors I had banged my head against my whole life—in my personality and in all the relationships and in everything else—persisting in some form. Here I was, finally free to walk in the bliss of eternal life with my Shepherd, yet hobbled with a resistant will holding fast, much like the mud still globbed across my legs after exiting from a refreshing dunk in the pond.

To this day, long after I had learned all the biblical basics of my belief, well beyond experiencing relief from the revelations of grace and identity in Christ, and even after I grasped more fully that this mud on me is not me, still the mud holds on.

I love the plea in Psalm 51:7, "Wash me, and I shall be whiter than snow." But I thought we did that already? Yes and no.

When I surrender, exactly what am I giving up? At the moment of salvation, I surrender my will and receive a life-giving Spirit joined to mine (did that). After salvation, I surrender that same will daily by allowing God to transform my soul till it aligns with His (learning to do that). And that means He aims to put to death everything in me not of God, namely, all those pesky old idols and failures of my flesh (now we're getting personal).

It seems accurate to say that this necessary, disagreeable surrender business—the act of giving up and laying down my will to the presiding control of the Spirit within me—is nothing less than the voluntary precondition to abiding in my identity in Christ. And since I'm fairly sure that didn't make sense, maybe this will: "Therefore I urge you, brethren, by the mercies of God, to present your bodies a living and holy sacrifice, acceptable to God, which is your spiritual service of worship" (Romans 12:1).

I'm made for it. I'm a fool not to do it. And when I stubbornly resist, God waits patiently with inextinguishable love for me to give in. And waits and waits.

———

"I thought I would be better by now" is a recurring thought with me. I have come to accept that there is not enough time left to have it all sorted out before the end. And as I write that, another car image from the past pops into my head (what can I say, I spend a lot of time behind a wheel). I'm driving across the vast open country of the flat Midwest. I see a car far in the distance, approximately even with me, and on a parallel path converging upon mine. I wonder who will get to the point of our merger—a mile hence—first. I admit to pressing harder on the gas pedal. But the closer we get, the more I realize the other car is going to beat me anyway, with ease. Turns out it was never going to be close.

My perspective is simply not as reliable as I make it out to be. With each passing year, just when I think I've made exemplary progress in my journey of faith, I'm surprised by more unseemly thoughts and behaviors, conveniently unnoticed before, which I've yet to turn over to God. I see a mile-long row of foibles that will beat me to the end. That used to bother my perfectionistic side, back when I had hope that some modicum of perfection was achievable in this life. But I realize that no matter how hard I try, perfection isn't going to happen for me on this earth. Not to worry. That was never the goal anyway; growing closer with Jesus—perfection personified—was always the goal, and the worthwhile reward. And death to my stubborn flesh (gulp!) is how I will get there.

I'm trying to explain all this as straightforwardly as I can. In fact, I've purposely avoided technical words like "sanctification" (which is what this is all about by the way). But the truth is I'm bungling the task. My mind plainly—or is it my plain mind—cannot comprehend the full extent of how this matter of death to my flesh must unfold. Only the heart is big enough to take it in, and mine is telling me something important: At some level I have not yet grasped the abject futility of resisting God in all the areas of my life. I'm simply not mature enough. Instead, I waste precious time trying all the usual escapist ways or, supposedly better, pleading, "Lord show me what to do to find my rest!" But that's just a delay tactic. I already know what to do. I have to go to the cross.

It seems there's nothing I can do to outrun the inevitable death to my fleshly ways that God, in His love, has planned. And short of my physical death, they won't be conquered in one fell swoop. All the vices of my soul must be surrendered in turn. Some of the time it's easy; I only need to be shown the merit of making the change— "Yes, Lord, I agree that I'm (name vice here). Count me in!"—and I begin to change, even if only incrementally. But the big changes don't get made that way. I never face those with a brave and fervent, "Super duper! By all means, let's get rid of that!" Doesn't happen.

With the big things, I never come to the place of surrender. I'm brought to it through brokenness.

With all of this talk of surrender, death to the flesh, and now brokenness, you might think that going to the cross is a traumatic process (it's certainly not a knee slapper, I'll give you that). But who in the world would rather remain shackled to their flaws than gain their freedom? Apparently I would. Even though, ironically, it's resistance to the necessary changes in my life that has always caused me the most pain, while resignation to what God must do has provided the greatest relief.

"For to me, to live is Christ and to die is gain" (Philippians 1:21) is to be my motivating rallying cry. Why of course! Since the choice is clear, then absolutely I cry, "Uncle!" already. Or do I? The alternative—to resist and therefore to endure over and over a slow death—is what I usually choose. My immature reasoning is as follows: I can do just fine loitering on the periphery of giving in. I'll still make it through this life, have some good times, I'll influence a person or two along the way, and end up with God in Heaven, happily ever after either way. Sounds about right, with one caveat—I will have to struggle with my own burdens and forego the deepening relationship Jesus offers to me while I am here. Oh, that.

Yes, that. In fact, that relationship *is* why I am here, and why I won't ever be truly happy by putting anything ahead of Jesus. That's why my flesh must die daily. And that's helpful to know. Thomas Merton, the renowned twentieth-century Trappist monk, observed, "When I see my trials not as the collision of my life with a blind machine called fate, but as the sacramental gift of Christ's love...I realize that my suffering is not my own. It is the passion of Christ."[41] Indeed, that is the desirable, mature view.

Wretched good times, these trials of transformation, and so much the better conquered when I don't fight back.

Chapter 27

THE DOOR

The best way out is always through.

ROBERT FROST

I like funerals. Cemeteries too. An unhealthy fascination with death? Not at all—I hate that there is such a thing. I'm sure it's a fascination with life. Facing death helps me appreciate the brevity of this life and to anticipate the eternal life hereafter that promises so much more. Left to my own devices and without benefit of that perspective, I would either mask the pain I feel or push it all away. Yes indeed, contemplating death brings the zoom lens to my appointed span of life and has always been a great comfort to me. And you are beyond thrilled with our cheery start to the chapter, I'm sure.

Ecclesiastes says there is "a time to weep and a time to laugh" (3:4). Well, the gang's all here for the laughter part, but who wants to weep? No matter, we must resolve not to feel nothing in our pain, for that is a walking death. At times I dabble there—in the numb, as it were. I try to pretend no sorrow and so close myself off from living truly, which is dreadfully sorrowful, prompting me to pretend, and so on. It is a troubling pattern. However, thankfully, there is a way out. It's not the way of less pain, it's just the better way.

I seemed to get that in a secular sort of way before I was a Christian, at least in one area of my life. My wife and I both wanted to have four children. I hesitated at first, aware that I was multiplying my chances for more difficulties. But I also recognized I wanted to live a full life. Give me multiple hardships if you must (whoever you are), but multiplication of happiness as well. In this life they are intertwined. Turns out I conquered my indecisiveness and had four dear children and my calculations proved to be correct.

Now it's many decades later, and sadly I have regressed. These days I'm back to playing it safe in many of the big areas of life, missing out on experiences in my quest to find a nice cushy place to put my head down and rest. Maybe it's an age-related phase, or perhaps I'm recuperating from the shock and trials of life. Regardless, my play-it-safe strategy never works. I always manage to veer myself straight into life's tough spots, from where, sorry to say, I've been known to grouse at God for my troubles, or worse, accuse him of abandoning me.

I know the theologians are right when they say, "The Father didn't abandon Jesus on the cross," Whom, significantly, He placed there, "and He won't ever abandon you." I also understand the redemptive merits of Romans 8:18: "For I consider that the sufferings of this present time are not worth comparing with the glory that is to be revealed to us." But tell all this to my emotions who seem to feel they shouldn't have to endure any hardship right this second.

What is one to do? You can't explain away the pain and suffering. You can hardly explain it at all. And that's why it is to our mutual peril that I'm wading in—boldly, don't you think?—to talk of sad things. We may not like to think about it, but it is necessary if we're to be honest with ourselves. So hold on tight, take heart, and know that it gets good again.

I have known great physical pain, but not like some. There are those who have known worse. I have also known great sorrow, but again not like some. Perhaps not like you. Physical pain harms the body, but despair devastates the soul. There is no need to trudge through specifics here of guilt, or grief, or regret, though I see I'm trudging anyway. It is inescapable. Death by streaming tears comes in degrees to every man. Multiply that by the billions of souls who have ever lived, and we find Jesus, "a man of sorrows and acquainted with grief" (Isaiah 53:3) astoundingly, incomprehensibly there. It is because Jesus died for us that every one of those tears has already been redeemed. Better yet, because He rose, you and I will get to that nice cushy spot one day. It's called Heaven and it exists every bit as much as this earth, just as surely as God made the moon "the lesser light to rule the night" (Genesis 1:16, ESV).

Last night I observed the moon in wonder from a well-worn Adirondack chair, trusty retriever nearby and some contemptible ghosts, too. I sat for a long time taking in the scene and pondering life—philosophy's a full-time job you might know. Earlier I watched the large morphing shadow from a row of cypress trees as it advanced toward me at an alarming speed, which was all it took to bring out my wistful side. Next thing I knew, I was under the moon thinking of all that was behind me in this life and how fast I got to today, and then the bugaboos started—hurt, regret, and whatnot. I have my low moods, you see, my piddling thoughts. Though I never lose my way. Through the toughest stretches, my heart always knows the way back to God. Perhaps that's when it knows it best. It's a homing instinct. I've heard it said that suffering is an open door into the heart of God. If that's so, my door still works fine; it's just that the hinges are worn. And that's probably a line from a country song, or should be.

I'm aware that a better routine than staring into the night is to get up early and face east into the sweet smell of the day, and from there to think more often about what is ahead till all the ghosts flee. "A man reaps what he sows" (Galatians 6:7, NIV) after all, and it probably sounds like I'm prone to sowing these somber moods. But I have my great moods too—genuinely joyful ones. Anyway, I don't know that either experience is more or less than the average man's. And here, I would like to pause to make an excuse for myself: My low moods are not groundless. There is true evil in this world, bent on soul-dismantling mischief, and his name is Satan and his aim is to wreak havoc when and where he can, and that is heartbreaking to me.

How to explain this evil state of affairs? God gave man the gift of free will, then Adam and Eve were tempted in the garden and... and it's my folly to go on since we know the story well and I can't begin to do it justice. All I know is that when I read the Bible, I see that Satan's nights are numbered, that there is another scene behind these gloomy ones, and that, thanks to Jesus, we don't live in the times of the shadows anymore; we live in the times of the dawn. Though in my downcast moods—like the one last night—it doesn't feel that way.

Most times when I get in my car, I reflexively reach for the radio first thing. I switch it on hoping to hear the words, "O-o-h child things are gonna get easier."[42] But I hear, "Good time Charlie's got the blues" instead.[43] That works fine for me, too, because I know why I'm reaching. We're all reaching for something, are we not? I for one have built a lifetime of habits for the same central purpose—to rid a certain feeling. And make no mistake, there is a feeling, difficult to pin down, yet born out of the toughest parts of life we all experience—relational disappointments, sickness and death, heartache, flat out beat up and worn down by a pretty mean world. And when I disagree with what I just wrote and call it "overblown," or "wallowing," all I have to do is make a list of hurts. It would be really long.

But impressions to the contrary, I'm not a walking sad sack muttering on about the meaninglessness of it all. Nor am I an alarmist perpetually warning that the sky is falling. I'm just an ordinary sojourner vacillating between two extremes of reality—first, that there is in fact a terrible and presiding gloom after the Fall, and second, that that gloom has been perforated fatally by eternal bright spots of life which bear a stunning resemblance to what lies ahead. Of these two, I'm naturally drawn to the latter, being an optimist at heart—who likes funerals, go figure. But it's true. Even with my sports teams—none of which have won a championship in years—I am a "We'll get 'em next year, guys," guy. And with that it seems I've stumbled onto a good analogy for the dour circumstances of our world. Miracles do happen, and a really big one is due!

Open up that sky, Lord, and come down here and reign already! Or take me home, one!

Not yet, I see.

The pains and joys of life are linked. You can't talk about one without the other. My sports teams may never win the big one while I walk this earth, but it does me no good to only see the pessimistic side ("We always lose!"). That's a welcome change in me, for that's exactly what I used to do in most areas of my life. It was my way of preparing for the worst so I wouldn't have to feel the disappointment. Eventually I found out that being a curmudgeon was an even worse feeling.

Living for joy will always outclass running from pain. Easier said than done, I get it. Life's hard and I take up no quarrel with myself or anyone else who's in a present struggle and sees the glass as half empty. But when it comes to God there's ultimately no room for pessimism, and I remind myself of that daily. So back and forth like a pendulum I go. Optimism. Pessimism. And today optimism wins! I have my go-to cheers for the purpose: the sun'll come up tomorrow; the good guys win in the end; "the LORD is my rock and my fortress and my deliverer" (Psalm 18:2). Though I do grumble.

I just can't help myself (and the pendulum swings back). I mean, look at this place! Even if your day is going swimmingly well, there is trouble about. How can anyone pretend otherwise?

I've known some people (translation: I've done the following) who, when you ask, "Is there anything I can pray about for you?" answer, "You know, there's really not, it's all good, business is booming, my petunias are blooming, and the family is doing well. Yes siree! God has blessed me, and I'm a happy man"—all said without a hint of a smile.

Really?! Let me help you: "Your wife is estranged from her mother, your son is failing algebra, your neighbor lost his house, and you're wearing the wrong belt. Everything is not 'all good!' And by the way, don't you watch the evening news? No? Well, I'll give you that one, that *is* good. But do you at least struggle with impatience? Make *me* feel good! Tell me something here! No one's life is untroubled in this warped world." But I don't say any of that, because he already knows it on the inside.

To make our goal in life to breeze through unscathed speaks loudly and sadly of our capacity to push away pain and pretend we are unaffected. "I'm already in; I've accepted Jesus. Yes, there's degeneracy at every corner, there'll be bumps along the way, but no big whoop-de-doo, the Man Upstairs will make sure things go smoothly for me. Just being an optimist, right?" Right. I mean wrong! The spirit of that thought is dead wrong! That I ease through this life isn't God's objective; my changed heart is, which He seems intent on shaping, much to my discomfort, through the despair and hardships of life.

"Happy people rarely look for joy," writes Larry Crabb. "They're quite content with what they have."[44] Nailed it! Happiness is not enough! I want Jesus to come back right now, and nothing short of His return will ever mollify my soul. I'm a sheep happily grazing one minute, thinking the grass is what it's all about, until I realize I've lost sight of my Shepherd. Then I'm bleating like mad and I won't stop till He comes back, till I finally see His face and cannot possibly contain my joy. I don't want more of the world; I want more of Jesus! And sure as lightning, He's coming.

Sometimes I feel all but inconsolable for those who won't believe in God. They have neither explanation nor hope for their secret miseries. At best they have temporary relief, denial by any other name. Yet for those of us who recognize and admit that the pain we're in is because we are broken people living in a broken place, we know God by name and call out to Him, "Father if there is another way..." even though we know there isn't. For there are still lost souls to reach, and we are still here learning to let His Spirit reign through us for that purpose. And knowing all that, I have no good excuse not to experience joy here and now in the waiting; just a deep-rooted one. My hurting soul won't let me.

In my soul I have my nadir-of-faith moments, where the thought flashes through, "If God cares so much about me, why won't He....whatever?" Yes, I have been hurt that badly and so have you. I have everything I need, yet there have been times I've sensed my Shepherd left me alone to graze. Then what I have is no longer enough. That's when faith gets tested. That's when well-meaning advice doesn't work. That's when I face a long stone wall.

Recently, very recently, I was deep in the hurting, until some dear friends had the love and wisdom to know what to do. As believers we are a family in this journey together, and when one of us hurts, we all hurt. However, I'm not used to depending on anyone. It's one of my biggest weaknesses. Not wanting people to know I'm hurt is another. But my dear friends were having none of it. They circled me, prayed for me, doused me with compassion, and showed me through their hearts, until I could see again with mine, that although He was out of sight for a time, my Shepherd was alive and well.

Henri Nouwen speaks a great truth when he writes, "Still my own pain in life has taught me that the first step to healing is not a step away from the pain, but a step toward it."[45] I read through that thought again now and hear the voice of my Shepherd, though it's farther off than I would like: "I put these people there for you. Let them bathe your soul for once in your life, kiddo!" Then I take another step.

—⁓—

Mike is a friend of mine who experienced a great peace. And he is a family man of deep faith and calm demeanor who is no wimp. He wasn't supposed to still be alive. In 2004, Mike was diagnosed with an inoperable brain tumor. No doctor would touch it, so the prayers began. Finally, one doctor on the west coast was found who said he'd do the surgery, and Mike was flown out for a ten-hour emergency procedure to cut that lousy tumor out. The prognosis was grim, but the prayers continued, and months of grueling treatment followed. We've all been touched by the routine and we know it's hard, but Mike is a trooper and he started to improve. During his recovery, one day I was surprised when he asked if I would drive him to our monthly men's group. He still wasn't well enough to drive himself, not by a long shot, but said he had missed the fellowship and book studies. Our entire drive there he never complained of his hardship tour, not one "woe-is-me." I would have been too scared to leave the house. Mike is my hero and a better man than I.

Years later, back to health—praise God—and still the better man, Mike shared something in our men's group that I've never forgotten. Nor did it escape me that in all our years of friendship it was the first time I had heard him complain, if you want to call it that: "I miss the closeness I felt with God when I was going through all that hell on earth." Then looking right past us and through the room to eternity, he added, almost mournfully, "I really miss Him."

Mike had found the "peace of God, which surpasses all understanding" (Philippians 4:7, ESV) that few of us ever find in this life. When a few minutes later he told us, "I'm so ready to go," and,

"I'm looking forward to it," it hit me that his words reflected those of a man no longer idolizing this life, but instead living for the life to come. He was free.

Mike told me recently that there has never been a feeling that compares to what he experienced back then, when his faith was so strong it was like a portal, deeper than intellectual knowing. Through that portal he would often come to meet with God Himself. And there, he came to understand more fully than he ever imagined that Jesus is as real as you and me; that He is the greatest joy in this life and in the life to come, even—no, especially—in the midst of our deepest pain.

As if that wasn't enough hope to take in for one day, he shared another experience that has stuck with me. Whereas those of us who prayed for him saw mostly pain and challenge, he saw beacons—that was his word—beacons, continually sent by God to light his path. When he was down, running out of hope, there was always someone, a nurse, a friend, or a stranger in the hospital lobby, who locked eyes and spoke into his soul in ways and with a timing that could only be explained if these encounters were foreordained. Fellow Christians, and perhaps some angels, were drawn together by God as one family to protect their own, to make sure Mike could lean in to their comfort and move on.

In the Book of John, Jesus says, "I am the Light of the world; he who follows Me will not walk in the darkness, but will have the Light of life" (8:12). Ever since Mike's supernatural encounters with his beacons, I've been more alert to recognize how God has provided the same in my life. Although I've been spared the severity—and blessing, Mike would say—of his ordeal, when I survey my life, I can spot a multitude of beacons, past and present. And I'm surprised to find—though I suppose I shouldn't be—that when I connect each shining one, I'm tracing the course of my journey. That is immensely encouraging to me. For it tells me that when I come to my next challenge, beyond what I can now see, there will be beacons waiting.

Part Seven

INTO THE HEART

Chapter 28

TRAVELING THROUGH

Earth's crammed with heaven,
And every common bush afire with God;
But only he who sees, takes off his shoes,
The rest sit round it and pluck blackberries.

ELIZABETH BARRETT BROWNING

My two favorite times of the day are when the sun first cracks through like flaming javelins and when its last glinting slivers flame out in a breath. It's enough to make one break out in rhyme almost.

I marvel at the sun, but wonder why I take for granted the less spectacular. What makes unkempt brambles ordinary to me, but the hatching robins within extraordinary? There's beauty in both, and it takes looking through God's eyes to see it. I like the rain, but not the gray skies; apparently I prefer my events dramatic.

Shallow thought. What event isn't? I regularly walk my path past the brambles and into the woods and submerge into the blue-green tinge till the serenity of nature enfolds me. And there I go gushing all poetical again. But the walk is heavenly while it lasts, and I am inclined to connect with God's heart when and where I can. Yet these interludes must end, for I live in a world where eventually I must come out to contend with what God puts in front of me— out where the challenging objective is to not be worldly.

Once I shared with a friend—a clear-cut extrovert—about why I moved out to the country and how much I enjoyed my long walks through the woods there.

"Why would you do that?" he asked, as he stared dumbfounded toward the woods. "I mean, what's there?"

"You mean besides God?" I thought.

I t's true; I'm an unrestrained nature lover, who sees no point in hugging trees. I'll marvel at them, take care of them, but I won't worship them. Only God, the Creator of those trees, is worthy of that. I well-realize, however, that there are some who have a different view: Father Time met Mother Nature and after a brief fling had an offspring called Earth. That is the essence of our origins if I'm understanding the God-skeptics correctly, and more specifically those scientists who revere the cosmos and worship the ground we walk on, literally, while dismissing the God of the Bible as mere fairy tale. I heard a preacher on the radio once say, "It doesn't seem that the Christians are the ones believing in fairy tales—this idea that atoms burst from nowhere and the earth was formed, and out of the water crawled a mudfish which turned into a frog and ultimately into a man. The last time I heard, a frog turning into a prince *was* a fairy tale."[46]

The skeptics will stop at nothing to deny God. It's not a matter of the evidence, the facts, or science; it's a matter of the heart and will. Or in their case, the "won't."

Begin tirade.

I used to believe the following, in turn, because "they" said so: the big bang theory (the universe popped into existence all by itself), the steady state theory (the universe has always existed), the oscillating universe theory (the universe pops in and out of existence), the multiverse theory (the more complex the theory, the more we can just make it all up), chaos theory (that speaks for itself), and the I-don't-have-a-clue theory (which gets my vote as their most promising option).

How scroungingly desperate they—the so-called "scientific community," which tellingly excludes input from most God-fearing scientists—must be to explain the ultimate origin of all things without so much as a wink toward an intelligent Creator. They actually know very little of stars and planets in their otherwise bright minds, and even less in their hearts because they discount Who made these to start. A single question from God, "Where were you when I laid the foundation of the earth?" (Job 38:4) and their snooty theories are undone.

I may not be much of a scientist, but in my mind and heart I know at least two facts about the universe: 1) "In the beginning God created the heavens and the earth" (Genesis 1:1) and 2) the stars in the heavens are countless and the sands of the sea beyond measure (Jeremiah 33:22). For purposes of science, last time I was at the beach I calculated that I washed off a million grains of sand every time I jumped into the ocean, which oddly, as far as I could tell, wasn't in the process of rising to flood the continents like I had heard (see chants of "climate change" for reference). I apologize for being snarky, but that little drumbeat is also part of their patter, is it not? That we must save planet Earth. Here's a news flash! It's not going to happen.

Turns out, these scientists are over their heads with something, and it's not rising seas; it's pseudoscience, claiming they know more than they do. Methinks they telleth whoppers. On second thought, I don't apologize.

I've had some washout picnics on what were supposed to be sunny days. It seems the "experts" can't tell me with any degree of accuracy if it's going to rain tomorrow, and this with benefit of satellite images from space, genuine observational science, yet I'm supposed to believe they know our planet will burn to a crisp in 1.7 billion years. Do I hear 1.8? Soooold! to the nearest humanist. Or looking backwards, similarly, they like to claim they can accurately discern the times of the dinosaurs. Never mind that the ages bounce around by millions of years every time a new "peer-reviewed" article gets posted, notably, without benefit of the peers who disagree with their worldview assumptions. And, straightaway, the information gets disseminated by and for those eager to lap it up. I save the articles, and their fickleness is sobering.

A new chunk of hipbone from only God knows what is discovered in some sandstone and declared to be indisputably that of a *skepto-sapien,* two hundred thousand years old. We do the math and discern next year that it will be two hundred thousand and one. Yet that's never the case. Instead, a few years later we hear they've been hard at work and learned more now (those dear people, always studying for our benefit), and it's actually a one hundred and seventy thousand-year-old *neander-dubious* or some such.

Let me be clear if I haven't been already. I'm not buying any of what they're selling, undergirded as it is by their not-to-be-questioned presuppositions, which are that God is irrelevant or nonexistent. Land sakes, if I didn't know any better I'd think they were desperately trying to persuade me that the universe is all there is. So I play along, reductio-ad-absurdum style, to lay bare the upshot of their belief: If matter is all there is, there can be no objective meaning to life (i.e. transcendent purpose infused into the universe). If there is no objective meaning to life, neither they, nor I, matter. And if that's the case, why are they spending their time studying matter, with self-proclaimed noble purposes yet?

Perhaps a thought experiment will bring them to their intellectual senses. According to their own latest accounts, the universe is expanding and is going to continue to do so until eventually, 2.8

billion years hence (author's note: margin of error 100 percent), all the stars turn out their lights and the party's over. With those pleasantries in mind, sit back, relax, and close your eyes—after reading the following would be best—and think of what that would be like. Let's begin: Think darkness. I'm talking pitch black. Now darker. Darker still. By the way, if you're doing this properly you won't know when you get to the end of our experiment, because remember, you won't be there when it all dies out, nor will anyone or anything else. So just keep on going until you see the point, which is this: If these scientists are correct, mankind is in a mad rush toward oblivion. One day it will be as if we never existed.

What a loathsome experiment! My apologies. We won't do that again. We have other absurdities to consider.

If the universe began out of nothing and will end in the same, why are these same scientists so bent on colonizing Mars? Logically speaking, no good reason that I see. Philosophically speaking, perhaps beneath their facade, they sense that this earth is not our final home. Any way you look at it, they have some curious reasons for wanting to leave, and in looking to Mars as the cure-all, they merely trade one temporary home for another, if you want to call it a home. I can't for the life of me understand why anyone would want to leave our planet of green things for a brownish rock, already dead, all because they're afraid the planet we're on is going to one day become dead. Sorry universe worshipers, you can run but you can't hide. When Jesus comes back and the earth goes down in flames, so does the rest of creation, including you. And it will be as if all the beakers and Nobel prizes, not to mention the government grants to study spotted owls, were never here.

And on that note, thank you for your research, noble and objective scientists, humanists all. Your hypotheses and conclusions are summarily rejected! How could I in good conscience do otherwise, given that your "objective" interpretations conspicuously leave the possibility of God out of the equation? Whatever you do, Dorothy, don't for one second look behind the curtain. With that as your starting point, you are no longer the empirical, unbiased scientists you make yourselves out to be, but instead philosophers who have strayed wide of the mark. I know poor philosophy when I hear it.

Sound philosophy, on the other hand, takes into account that we all have presuppositional worldviews. The Christian begins with the assumption that God created nature. "For since the creation of the world His invisible attributes, His eternal power and divine nature, have been clearly seen, being understood through what has been made, so that they are without excuse" (Romans 1:20). But to the pseudoscientists, nature is the beginning and the end-all, a closed system, though he can't prove that empirically. Watch him squirm as he tries. Even so, he's not deterred. He's actually rather proud. With apologies to poet Joyce Kilmer, "I think that I shall never see a god as lovely as a tree," is the apropos starting point for all aspiring pseudoscientists. And what a grim worldview it represents, since according to their own science, a tree amounts to nothing more than a future dead thing.

Here at last, we arrive at our common ground with these mistaken, intelligent men of science—the planet and all the trees and oceans, and let us not forget the owls, will surely meet their demise, just not for the reasons the skeptics say. It won't be caused by poor stewardship of the planet, but by man's original rebellion toward God, the One that set in motion the inevitable fact that at some point none of us will get to enjoy this future earth. Though not to miss is that a multitude will indeed get to enjoy the new one. The Bible hasn't deviated one iota from that fact. Perhaps these scientists could research that.

Our friendly pseudoscientists are not making these inroads by working alone. They proclaim as fact, "Blah, blah, blah" (it does tend to run together after a while), then change a year later to contradictory blah-blah that the fawning media, all willing and credulous, propagate as scientific fact.

And I think we can all agree that most informative of the propaganda are those well-balanced documentaries that go out of their way to teach us that Jesus is a myth. These are often on the same television stations, mind you, that spend untold dollars contriving documentaries saying that Hitler escaped and moved to South America, that there has been yet another discovery of a hidden secret gospel of the Bible—factual representations of who, what, when, or where are beside their point; and we already know why—and most helpful of all, exposing the truth that space aliens are our ancestors, one of whom we've stashed away in a hangar in the desert, which might make the rest of them return any minute to

harvest us for Sunday dinner (seems right). But that the God of
the Bible created the universe and life and you and me? Don't be
ridiculous! The experts won't have it. "Only narrow-minded, weak
people lean on such a crutch in an attempt to tell us how to live
our lives by making up a being who is supposedly sovereign over
man. How dare you!"

How dare I not?

I make no exclusive claim to the moral high ground. I used to
be a skeptic and do what skeptics do—push away the truth that
a Supreme Being chose to make this place. So I get where they're
coming from. But back in those days, even at my rebellious worst,
there was always a part of me that acknowledged I needed more. I
was miserable without Him.

Not so the God-averse skeptics. They seem to revel in playing
make-believe. "God is dead," pronounced the atheist philosopher
Friedrich Nietzsche, and our pseudoscientists and their ogling co-
horts are inclined to agree. "Let us discount the Bible and disavow
the possibility of God before we begin, shall we?" And in the end
what do they prove? Nothing. Which might be their point. We as
Christians, however, know that the only reason there is anything at
all is that there *is* a God, thus proving that at least there is a possible
way for man to have everything. Which is decidedly our point.
Wait! What did I just say?

I said this: Let them pretend to inform each other and let us
stop scaring ourselves over their dubious computations. Man hurtling through space on a future fireball is not the problem; hurtling
headlong into the last days of the end times is. And pseudoscientific

balm to help the skeptics avoid thinking about the personal consequences of those end times won't change a thing. They'll be moving
through the chapters of Revelation along with the rest of us whether they acknowledge it or not. All the conditions and prophecies
and nations converging to these times, to a single point of the end
times, they can't stop. In fact, their denial is part of the equation.
God told us it would happen (2 Peter 3:3-4).

All of this explains a thing or two about our increasingly godless society. The colluding skeptics and the deliberately gullible put
on a united front. But at some point each day, each person sits in a
favorite chair at home on a continent of the globe in a far corner of
a galaxy in the middle of nowhere and must fashion meaning from
the future cold, dark place they've imagined. And since that can't
be done while retaining one's sanity, all that's left is a hard paddle
upstream to promote or compel some worldwide ethos centered on
creation that will supposedly come to the rescue. Only one problem: the body of Christ is alive and well, and that unsettling fact
doesn't fit their "godless" theories. Hence, their diabolical solution
is underway across the globe—to relativize truth so as to marginal-
ize Christians. And vice versa.

It's sheer madness, and I'm quite sure they want to put us out
of their misery. For this purpose the megaphones have been given
to the skeptics, and society's unraveling is the aftermath.

As a one-nation-under-God patriot, I'd love nothing more
than to see the reemergence of this once-great country so we can

influence the world back to where it needs to be. "Never say die," they say. But the reality is that most days frustration and helplessness over what appears a losing battle to rediscover true science, regain our culture, and right our government get the better of me. Then, in my good moments, I remember this country was never supposed to be nirvana anyway. Why would it be? It has the same fatal wound as the rest of the world. Patriotism is needed, but it is a poor substitute for an exorcist.

Underneath my fears, I know all the propaganda and shenanigans are the smoke and mirrors of an unseen war—one that God's children are fated to win. For that reason, we have the least reason to feel helpless. Where I think I see a defeat, God sees another victory. In the end, only He knows where the real blows fall. But one thing I do know: The body of Christ has been present in this nation from day one, and it will live on long after this nation and this world are gone. Till then, all who are His do what we can, even as we wait in a far corner of a galaxy for His return and final victory. And I think sound science supports me on that.

End tirade.

The earth-worshiper fancies himself a man of compassion: "I'm okay with the fact that I'll die one day so long as precious Mother Earth lives on." But his claim is bluster, spoken to justify misplaced allegiance, and it goes against every eternal fiber of man. Earth to skeptics! I have a soul. The earth does not; it is—brace yourselves—soulless!

Knowing that it is soulless, I still respect and appreciate this earth and don't take lightly that during my brief time here I have the privilege of caring for the earth to the glory of the one true God Who made it (Genesis 1:26). And here is a good place to allay my guilt and make amends to Mr. Kilmer and his sublime work of art: "Poems are made by fools like me, but only God can make a tree." How about that! A God-adoring poet speaks more truth than all the pseudoscientists and earth-worshipers combined. My heart rallies. And my tirade has ended, now for a second time.

I don't know how many days I have left to walk this earth. Going by the seasons, I'm in waning autumn, but can only surmise.[47] It is a good season. With each passing year I grow more fascinated by the beauty and design of this wonderful planet. I am a nature lover at heart indeed. Of course every Christian is, for in the most honest sense he takes into account Who created nature in the first place. The humanist conveniently ignores the obvious and covets the earth for himself.

Here's hoping one day if he sees a burning bush it will get his attention.

—⁓—

Sometime, somewhere, unbeknownst to me, a gray squirrel ran up a tree and sent a leaf spiraling down past a small insect beating its wings. The leaf dawdled downward and settled upon a stream, then floated through a meadow nestled under billowy clouds and a golden sun that shines on me. I skip a rock—as I like to do—and marvel at the leaf drifting by, and at the God Who saw it all and sees me. A veritable splendor it is. But the most inspiring part is that it doesn't hold a candle to Heaven.

Chapter 29

HOME

All things on earth point home in old October;
sailors to sea, travellers to walls and fences, hunters
to field and hollow and the long voice of the hounds,
the lover to the love he has forsaken.

THOMAS WOLFE,
OF TIME AND THE RIVER

I think about Heaven every day.

Once, after listening to a sermon on the rapture, I asked a nearby pew-mate if he thought there would be a great variety of things to do and see in Heaven. I'm strange that way.

"We'll be too busy worshiping God to care," he replied, "and beyond that we can't know and shouldn't speculate."

"Uh-huh. Well, have a nice day." Really, that's all I said. "Have a nice life!" I realized would have been too caustic, as would, "Listen brother, I'm already a citizen of Heaven (Philippians 3:20) and an ambassador for it while I'm here on Earth (2 Corinthians 5:20). And while I agree that everything we do in Heaven will have the quality of worship, I'm not sure you and I are defining worship the same way. Furthermore, it's not 'speculation,' it's called imagination. So if it's all the same to you, I will imagine to my heart's content. Though to be clear, no man not named Jesus Christ has ever come close to imagining the splendor that God has in store. And by the way, we're getting a new earth—you might have read that somewhere—so doesn't it figure to be at least as full and fantastic as the current one? And do you know what else? Only a spiritual bully would try to rain on someone else's spiritual parade. Since I was a young child I've imagined what Heaven will be like and I'm not stopping now."

But like I say, that would have been too caustic, so I just eased my irritated self away.

Speaking of limited imagination, for a long time I had a mental list—these days it's commonly called a "bucket list"—of all the things I wanted to do in this world before I die. It was not an unusual list: see the Natural History Museum in London, take in a rainforest or two, run with the bulls in Pamplona (that was from my younger days; scratch that one), go on an Alaskan cruise, or maybe even skydive (scratch that one too). But you get the general idea.

More recently, I was reflecting on how I've never done any of those things and on how worn and crinkly my list had become—nothing new added in years. It's not as if my interests have waned. I can think of new ones on the spot (let's see, if I die today, it would mean among other things that I never got to learn to play the guitar well, throw a credible spiral, or become remotely proficient at anything mechanical). Rather, I stopped adding to the list because after all these years of striving, and in the face of eternity and all the wonders that await, I'm finally content with my glaring mound of non-accomplishment.

I'm not saying I don't want to live life to the fullest while I'm here on Earth, just that even when I do it won't begin to scratch the surface of all available experiences anyway. There will always be thousands upon thousands of things I didn't do to dwarf the few hundred I did. Not to mention, this world is brimming with options, but it is also vast. I can choose to spend my lifetime catching planes to far-off spectacles, or I can walk in my backyard and see miracles every day. There's no rush. That's all I'm saying.

An acquaintance who retired with comfortable means once shared with me that he passed up the chance to get the car of his dreams—a Mercedes—reasoning that if he bought it he wouldn't be able to look forward to the anticipation of having it anymore. He understood that the dream was sufficient, and I agreed with his line of reasoning.

I have no desire to be an ascetic homebody. That's its own trap. If God inspires me to climb Mt. Everest—please no! In Jesus' name, amen—then I should climb the mountain, if for no other reason than to experience His joy through the process. But if inspiration doesn't strike, not experiencing the climb doesn't mean I have under-lived. "You only have one life, might as well live it up," I often hear. Yeah, one life, that for the Christian so happens to last for eternity, where a trillion years will be too small to measure.

In the Sermon on the Mount, Jesus told the disciples, "Do not store up for yourselves treasures on earth...But store up for yourselves treasures in heaven...for where your treasure is, there your heart will be also" (Matthew 6:19-21). I don't recall Him adding, "And by all means make sure to check off another adventure today on good ol' planet Earth." Similarly, Paul wrote to Timothy and advised him to enjoin "those who are rich" to store up "the treasure of a good foundation for the future, so that they may take hold of that which is life indeed" (1 Timothy 6:17,19). And although there is a live-it-up-now part of me that doesn't offer a peep of an amen, I pay it no heed. In my heart the message is loud and clear: Don't live as if this is all you get. Peep to that. But tell that to the masses who spend untold dollars chasing the fountain of youth so they can experience yet more of what Earth offers while ignoring the inevitable—they too will die.

I'm no forbearing saint, delaying the gratification found in bucket-list experiences due to my laser-focus on how much more God has in store—although I'd like to be. The reality is that most days, amidst the challenges of life, I lose the clear vision of the heavenly picture ahead. I wish I could see more, but admittedly, smack in the middle of my ambassador tour, certain barriers always muddle the view.

As I've said, my grandmother was the first person close to me who died. She was a colorful personality who had a beauty of soul and presence, and I loved her dearly. I don't remember much about her memorial service, other than the part where the pastor spoke about a caterpillar turning into a butterfly. It was clear what he was getting at, but I couldn't see how the pastor would know this about my grandmother. He'd never met her. I could only hope he knew something I didn't.

Two years after she passed away I became a Christian, and soon began to wonder where she ended up. As far as I could tell, she never gave any indication of accepting Christ, and no relative or acquaintance could tell me anything that gave me hope otherwise. Only God did that, when He spoke to my heart and said, "You have no way of knowing how I can reach each person with the message of My love." I like to think He shared that to let me know that when she was in a coma, nearing the end, Jesus came to her in her unconscious state and proposed, and in the recesses of her heart and mind, she accepted. Then again, maybe God just shared that with me so I wouldn't make myself the final judge of things I can't know. Either way I come to the same place on the matter: "It is for the Lord to 'search the heart and test the mind' of every man" (Jeremiah 17:10, ESV).

Still and all if someone tells me today they have no interest in Christ, I'd be a fool not to take him at his word and begin some serious praying on his behalf, as well as to keep alert for opportunities to engage him in friendly, meaningful discussion. I wish I knew all that before Grandmother died. But like I say, I cant judge what I can't know.

Nor can I dictate the outcome. There will always be some people, no matter what, who will say, "Not interested, Jesus," and willingly, inconceivably, choose Hell.

Hell—a place horrible by any definition. Here's mine: A self-chosen, godless, loveless, spaceless, timeless trek to oblivion that never quite gets there, where an ever-decreasing soulishness is all there is. On the subject of man's free will and Hell, C.S. Lewis wrote, "I willingly believe that the damned are, in one sense, successful, rebels to the end; that the doors of hell are locked on the inside."[48] I think he's right. Heaven is the good in every way, but given every opportunity, certain people will eternally say no. And apparently they needed to be here on Earth to have the freedom of their own poor choosing. I know in Heaven God will comfort my soul with the right perspective, but while I'm still here, it's the toughest part of the whole deal.

The pain and suffering in this life are the next toughest. I crave a clear perspective on why it has to be like this. For every good I see in this life, there seems to be even more suffering, and no getting around any of it. It's hard to get over. But I know the day is coming when I won't be dwelling on the brokenness of this current life any more, a day everything Satan did to rip us all off will be righted. "Blessed are those who have been persecuted for the sake of righteousness, for theirs is the kingdom of heaven," (Matthew 5:10) promised the crucified, dead, and buried Lord Jesus Who got up and walked out of His grave! And therein lies the answer of all answers for the perspective I seek: I will be resurrected as well (John 6:40)—if not first raptured—into the Kingdom of Heaven. This life on Earth is not the end.

As I think of that now, a fog lifts and my imagination runs straight to my future home and all that it could be. I like to think of it as my Heaven List.

—◊◊◊—

A Treasury of Heaven
(note: my view will differ from yours)

I believe at a future time I will stand before God, and it will be... How do I put a word on a feeling I've never experienced? Beats me, though one word keeps coming to mind—"rapturous." Yet that's not the right one because I might have been raptured already, in which case the word must describe a feeling beyond rapturous. Perhaps I'll feel meta-rapturous. No, that sounds cliched. Supra-rapturous? Tongue twister. Parapturous? That's the word! Tell 'em you heard it here first.

In my parapturous state, my Heavenly Father will shower me with great love and abounding kindness, and waves of happiness will restore my soul as He tells me over and over what I've longed to hear all my life: "Well done, son, well done."

Eyes cast downward, I'll say, "But Father I've made many mistakes and done a lot of bad things."

He will then put His gentle hands on either side of my face and turn my gaze to meet His—a countenance beyond beautiful—"All things have been made new, son."

And I'll notice for the first time that Jesus is standing beside me, smiling with victory in His eyes, and power. In that moment the whole of my life will make sense and I'll know that all the mistakes, sorrow, and worry of my life have melted away for good.

At once the Holy Spirit will enwrap my soul with His consuming love and I'll understand that I'll never need any substitute for that love again. I'll see His love as a "river of the water of life, as clear as crystal, flowing from the throne of God and of the Lamb" (Revelation 22:1, NIV), and through me and every heart that is His on Earth, and right through the hearts of Heaven into eternity. "This is not your run of the mill day," I'll be thinking. After all that, the reunions will begin.

And here in mid-muse the picture already grows fuzzy as the plain, practical questions of life emerge. When I sit at the marriage supper of the Lamb and drop my napkin on the floor, will I be embarrassed or will Jesus and I have a good laugh instead? Will I take baths every night because I got dirty pulling weeds in the garden? Will there be weeds? When I fly my kite will it sometimes get caught in the trees or crash onto the ground, and if so, will that be part of the fun? In other words, will I recognize the common parts of life as I know them now, or will it all be a new experience beyond what I've ever known or dreamed? I say, "Yes to all that is good!" And that means my elbow won't hurt anymore, or my knees, and that all my drives will mostly go straight, that "boredom" won't be a word, or "stress," and that at least some of my jokes will be worth laughing at. "Yes! Yes to all!"

Suddenly this stream of thought doesn't sound reverential enough. I guess I've heard so often that one should only speak of God in spiritual tones befitting His glory, that a bit of guilt creeps in after all. But I reject that baloney outright. There's no need for guilt for expressing a heart full of gratitude and excitement for all that Jesus has done and will do. He is not some detached foreign king. He is my gracious King and He has the heart of a giver, and eternal life with the King of kings is the ultimate gift, and my gratefulness is a blessed reward. How's that for spiritual tones?

And with conscience cleared, onward I dream of benevolent angels and rolling green meadows and such:

"Truly I say to you, today you shall be with Me in Paradise," (Luke 23:43) Jesus told the thief on the cross. My appointed day is coming as well. And when I'm there, I believe I will talk with Jesus as my friend, and I will delight in His wisdom, and experience daily "how wide and long and high and deep is the love" He has for me (Ephesians 3:18, NIV). And loving Him back will be my favorite thing to do.

I believe I will share the company of all the loved ones in Jesus who preceded me and, in the blink of an eye, all those who are going to follow. And the great gathering from the four corners of this present world will hold its share of surprises for me, and everyone there will be the dearest of family.

I believe that through all the great celebrations and love for each other, it will never be overwhelming, but always relaxed and comfortable in every way. We will care for each other above all and never have need to put our guard up. There will be no more unsanctified flesh, no more loss, no more death, no more pain. Because God always wins.

That is why I believe God's original plan for His children, this earth and all its beauty and variety of animals and natural spectacles, and so much more will be fulfilled in Heaven. We'll have a new earth that far exceeds the current one, but it will be familiar in all the important ways. It will have bright blue skies and grassy fields of colors I've never seen, colors of joy and love. And we'll enjoy every bit of the new creation and take care of it as perfect stewards this time, with skill and excellence, and we'll rejoice in how much it makes God smile.

I believe all my dogs will be there, making God smile as well. Sometimes I think of all the dear dogs I've loved so much—maybe a dozen at this count—and seen die always too soon. And though they don't have spirits and so have no chance of doing what only a man can—accepting Christ as Savior and knowing Him in the same union as do we—they do have souls. And I believe God will reanimate these dogs and a host of other animals and creatures so that the fullness of nature will be there for our stewardship and enjoyment, and no doubt for His as well. Yes, I believe there will be barking in Heaven. And for those who say, "We'll be so happy with God's presence that we won't care if our dogs (and other pets) are in Heaven," I say, "We'll be so enamored with God and He with us, that He'll make sure they are there. I believe I will be swarmed over by twelve wagging tails.

I believe in all these things not to conjure up whatever might temporarily comfort or suit my whims, certainly not to concoct things that would contradict Scripture, but because my Father put them in my heart to keep me steadfast throughout my journey and to remind me of all the doting He has in store. That's why I can no longer restrain the fervor of my praise. I believe too much in the extravagance of my list. I will not hold back anymore.

I believe serpentine streams will kiss through valleys of tall, bending grass on a scale that will make the verdant English countryside seem ordinary by comparison.

I believe there will be an awaiting Tree of Life whose welcoming branches easily surpass the restful laps of Earth's best grandmothers.

I believe there will be golden streets filled with happy people, and that there will be craftsmen, scientists, artists, and even writers—for there must be books!—working creatively, fully engaged in manifold endeavors of industry, all to the great joy of God and each other. All this will be done reflecting a tenderness, in a way that here on Earth we only partially do because we always hold back; there is always a part of us that does it for ourselves. But on the new earth everything will be done for God's glory. We will be unwound from our interfering flesh, and we will reach the heights of what we were created to be.

I believe there will be lingering talks and music and laughter and savory feasts and rests and walks, long pleasant walks with Jesus—because, as a matter of course, if your picture of Heaven doesn't include Jesus, you're not picturing Heaven yet.

Did I happen to mention this list has no end?

I believe gratefulness will overflow in Heaven. As will love.

And I believe there will be swooping hawks and cream-colored horses and gardens and songs and friendly ants and waterfalls and soft, ferny plants and stingerless bees…

I believe God gave men imaginations to point the way home.

Chapter 30

THE HEART OF THE MATTER

In all the important ways, I peaked in kindergarten. I had the blissful naiveté of the young optimist, reveled in carefree days of boundless interests, and had a soft cozy bed where I could lay my head down at night. As far as I was concerned, but for an occasional skinned knee, all of life was good, and the road ahead was destined to be untroubled. Turns out I was right, of course, if you skip over the prelude called "life on earth," where the fall of man means that suffering and death are part of the deal.

I found that out soon enough, but couldn't accept that that was the end of the story. "Happily ever after" was nonnegotiable to my way of thinking. And with that weighing heavily upon me, my carefree days eventually gave way to a subsuming line of inquiry: Who am I? Why am I here? And for that matter, what happened to that soft cozy place where I used to lay my head down? All collectively known as, "How do I fill the ache in my soul?" Thus began a lifelong quest to find the happy ending.

My mother often warned, "You can't go back, it's never the same." She was especially vocal about it during my teen years whenever my meaning-of-life pensiveness turned to grousing over my faded childhood. I've never regretted my pensiveness by the way, other than the time a kickball hit me in the face because I was pensively observing Debbie what's-her-name and contemplating the meaning of my love life. Mostly true. But as I say, I don't regret my ruminative ways—my comfort zone to sort myself and everything else out—for it led me through what appeared a pointless maze at the time, but turned out to be a thirty-six-year-long straight line to a formative insight: Man is lonely whether he admits to it or not, because something went horribly wrong and this place is not right, so he distracts himself by hiding in crowds, in himself, or both. Further, if he had to face it head-on he'd be too sad, for he can never live up to what he was supposed to be, this world doesn't measure up to what he needs it to be, and most bracing of all, there's no getting out alive...without Jesus that is. That was some doozy of an insight. No wonder I was forlorn for so long.

By the time I became an adult-acting person, I harbored a great unrest in the pit of my soul. It was a genuine fear that I was going to live and die without ever finding what this life was all about. I can't act like I was unswerving in my search during those times. I spent a profligate portion running from God and willingly being lured forth by the father of lies into the wide world of self-indulgence and false self-esteem, which in all its variations fits neatly under the heading, "What's in it for me?" In the end, I concluded if there's no God, nothing! But I took my sweet time to move on that insight, choosing the unwise courses of life first, and hence enduring a broad sweep of human pointlessness, false security, halfheartedness, restlessness, sadness, diversion, bored sillydom, frustration, confusion, fear of death, and hopelessness. I mean, who can hope in any of that? "The mass of men lead lives of quiet desperation," Thoreau once wrote.[49] I was noisy about mine.

By now you know the trajectory of my story. I had a good family and a good job, yet continued to stumble—providentially, forward—until my drive to find the truth and meaning of life converged in a love of books, a love of apologetics, and the love of two friends in the body of Christ who prayed me toward the light, where in a single decision in time, flickering hope became flaming faith and my heart was rescued from an ominous fate. Merciful Savior! My life had changed forever. And there you have it, my salvation story. No, wait! That's not quite it. My life didn't change. It was "exchanged" with a new eternal one. And angels had a party. Much better.

I found out right away that being a Christian was everything I had hoped for and surprising as could be. The biggest surprise was to learn that, in the perceptive words of one writer, "Salvation is so much more than a change of destination from Hell to Heaven! The true spiritual content of our Gospel is not just Heaven *one day*, but Christ *here and now*."[50] A close second was how I struggled all those years to be free of my unrest, thinking once I finally had my answer it would be an afternoon walk in the park. Instead I found I was free all right, free to struggle with a resistant soul that kicked and screamed its way through the ongoing lessons of surrender to the Holy Spirit within. And here and now I thank my Heavenly Father that He loved me too much to leave me the way I was, and here and now I thank my earthly father for the same reason.

Two decades have passed since my conversion, and I still find I'm as prone as ever to reminisce about the past. It's my escape from this present world, I suppose. In my most Pollyanna-ish moments I've imagined that the wandering parts of my soul would settle down if I lived in a simpler time and place. Perhaps if I were, say, a nineteenth-century hermitic alpaca herder in the Andes, and I kept my head down just so, the meanness and trivialities of the world would disappear into those mountains. But I know they wouldn't. Ecclesiastes 7:10 warns, "Do not say, 'Why were the old days better than these?' For it is not wise to ask such questions." I'm often unwise. I'd still be in a depraved world, wouldn't I? Same as now, where many people don't even care to ask, "Why am I here?" Significantly for me, I no longer ask that either. Now it's "How much longer before Jesus returns?"

And at once I see the real reason I reminisce in the first place.

In between my reflective moments, I still study like crazy, same as always, only now it's to grow closer to Jesus and to learn to be a better man. One thing I've learned is to listen more these days—which is a needed change—not only to God's voice, but to the wisdom He shares through my brothers and sisters in Christ. Their lived-out truths in all the stages and walks of life teach me to live better in my own.

I've also learned recently that I still make things too complicated. I received an email from a friend—somewhat younger than I—summarizing his experiences in his Christian walk: "Spending time with God means you get to know God better, and as you get to know him better you trust God more. As you trust God more, you love God greater, and the more you know, love, and trust God, the more you know how to rest in God; the more you rest in God, the more you learn to simply wait with patience and let him work it out. All of it. Right? I mean it ain't rocket science." He communicated about this subject as well and succinctly as I've ever heard, but I knew if I shared it with you from the start you might not read this book.

I admired his philosophical insights, even as it brought to mind the many lost souls who don't take the time to honestly consider the meaning of life—not that they would admit it if they did. It's sad and eminently prayer-worthy. Nevertheless, till they change their tune I'm not buying the pretense of their answers. Life that ends in a death of wishful thinking and nothing more borrows meaning from thin air. Our struggling society bears witness.

On the one hand, atheism and the bankruptcy of meaning it entails is being given a platform. On the other hand, we're told that all roads lead to God or some form of god thereof. By the looks of things, all roads apart from God lead to an unraveling. I suppose one could make a case that there are as many religions as there are men who in their own minds have a personal faith about life and why we exist at all. But faith is no better than the object in which it is placed. I can have faith that if I jump off a building, a host of butterflies will swoop in and carry me down to a soft blanket in the park where a picnic basket overflowing with a king's feast awaits. But when I jump, I will simply fall to the ground with unpleasant results. And even if the butterflies did catch me, it's unlikely they'd stage a very good picnic. My perception doesn't determine reality. God does. Every bit of it.

As you can see, I'm still an all or nothing person. Life is all about God or it's all about nothing. I've learned that there are no other options. I've also learned that the day is coming when the lights will go out in this country and all the others for good. The Good Book is clear about that. All things are moving toward an appointed showdown. We don't know when, but the season is nigh, and one day we're going to be surprised. Then it'll be all or nothing for sure. The time for men to decide where they stand is now.

Until recently my heart did not agree with my mother. Maybe for her the halcyon days of yore are best kept yore. But her childhood home is now a freeway on-ramp; she had to let it go. Mine is still there, as is my elementary school. They're just smaller. When I went back to Miami a few years ago, I walked my old neighborhood and moped around my school one Saturday afternoon, even looked through the cafeteria window and pictured where I used to sit around the lunch tables telling whoppers with my buddies. Some part of me was shocked that the tables were dead empty, and for the first time my heart understood: I can't go back. There are only two options—stagnant and forward. I know which of those is made for me, but admittedly, it can be hard sometimes to pick up my feet, particularly when I'm not hearing God like I should.

You see, though new in spirit, I still have many of the same foibles in my soul; they're just more worn in. I do believe I'm an improved version from that converted man who took those first wobbly steps and missteps. I certainly don't have all the answers yet—relatively few actually. But now I know Who does.

I still have many of the same preferences and interests, like sports—as a spectator but for a few passes at golf or shots at a basket in the driveway here and there. And you'll not be surprised I'm still a dog person. Ask any dog that's ever owned me and they'll tell you the same: "Woof!" "Well, I'm proud to be your person," I say back.

I still like the book where Dick and Jane visit their grandparents' farm, only now I'm the grandfather in the story, which is odd because inwardly I'm five. Maybe I was always the grandfather. Grandfathers have answers children need to know. Here it is, five-year-old me: Jesus Christ is the culmination of every good quest.

If only I had known that from the start. But of course I couldn't have. "Our lives are not puzzles to be figured out," observes author and scholar Eugene Peterson. "Rather, we come to God, who knows us and reveals to us the truth of our lives."[51] Which God continues to do for me in faith-affirming ways.

Not many years after leaving business for vocational ministry, a relative told me that she had happened to cross paths with the mother of a close friend from my youth. When she shared with her that I was now in full-time ministry, this woman—God bless her—who hadn't seen or heard from me since childhood, replied: "Knowing the Kevin I always knew, that doesn't surprise me one bit," which surprises me to no end every time I think about it. God is good to me.

And that is a good place to leave off. Though I'm tempted, the end of this story will not be the sentimental bow: And I lived happily ever after. That can only happen when absent from this body anyway, for when creation suffers, we all do. Instead, I will close the telling of my earthly sojourn in the eternal setting of its beginning: Why am I here? I exist because my great God chose to make me, astonishingly, so that I would in turn choose to enter an everlasting journey into His heart. That I have done. For that I am thankful. And that is the end of this story, but it is only the beginning of mine.

Afterword

The thought occurred to me midway through the writing of this book that I might get raptured before I finish. I admit to having a fleeting angst that that would be a shame, which is solidly on the pathetic side—an ill-conceived thought that only proves I still hold on to too many things of this world. "Say, God could you wait a bit? I'd like to finish this book first. At least hold off until after the playoffs this weekend." I have a short view of God at times. However, I write my admission of failure without shame, for I know it's not my final say. This is: Get lost feeble feelings and fleshly ways. I want what God wants. Period.

Writing this book has reminded me of one of our many family trips out West. I'd announce to the kids, "You see that mountain up ahead there, kids? We should be there in a few minutes." An hour later the mountain hadn't moved any nearer as far as I could tell. So too, the ending of this book was always in sight, but after a while it surprised me that it seemed no nearer. Then all of a sudden, "Hey, would you look at that! We're here!" Writing a book is not a quick jog around the block. It is a cross-country tour where you have plenty of time to reflect and observe along the way, and every thought has its proper time to marinate. It is the long view.

As I write this, the cat, whose own longevity is vexing, just came skittering across the hardwood floor because he's frisky due to the beautiful rain outside which I hear pattering on the broadleafed plants. I drift into the thought that this same water will be pouring into an ocean two hundred miles away. And that makes me think of how the hand of God touches my heart in a thousand ways all at once. Next thing I know I'm feeling grateful for that cat. But wait! I thought I didn't like cats.

And so it goes with all matters of the mind. My reasoning, I've learned, will take me only so far. One day I will surely be surprised when I cross Paradise's doorstep and all the in-between from birth till then will find its context and make sense. In the meantime, I'm a soul always writing on the inside. And by the looks of this book, a soul rambling some will say. But these aren't ramblings, I defend. They're the thoughts and feelings that patter like rain from a philosopher's mind—a glorified observer to some—who may not have gotten it all right, but who got it all true to his heart.

Some philosophers plumb the meanings of shadows on cave walls—quite brilliantly in fact[52] —though it never seems to go further than that. So why revere these men as the smartest of the smart when none are speaking of God? I've heard preschool children talking wisely about the God of the Bible. And speaking of children, I believe I was born with a writer's heart, and I think I knew that early on. However, it wasn't until much later in life that it occurred to me that I could have been a writer all those struggling, seeking years (My oh my, how I would have enjoyed that). Then I caught myself and realized I wouldn't have had anything to write about other than shadows. And you wouldn't have enjoyed that. I'm quite sure my heart wouldn't have been in it. Oh, I suppose I could have written faux-solutions to overcoming the meaninglessness of life, but to add to the crowded sea in the self-help section of the bookstore wasn't for me.

I began this book with a clear bias. I already knew why I was here: to receive God's love, to love Him in return, and to love others well. So my point of view by necessity traced my life experiences with love as its aiming point. All the years of seeking and hope and faith were seared into my heart, to be finally let out, no doubt for that purpose. That, by the way, is a good definition of a labor of love, and it reminds me of Jesus, how everything He does is for love, and how when we enter His heart we learn that we are loved eternally. If I did my job, that's what this book was really about.

There are times I question myself, "Isn't it presumptuous to think that I have something to say that might influence someone to travel deeper into the heart of God?" But it is actually more presumptuous to think I couldn't. After all, God is the One Who chooses to reach out to us, to relentlessly pursue us, even sometimes through ordinary books like these.

—KM

Notes

1. "No one can come to Me unless the Father who sent Me draws him; and I will raise him up on the last day" (John 6:44).

2. Song lyrics from "It Took a Miracle," John W. Peterson, Hill and Range Songs, 1948.

3. Sheldon Vanhauken, *A Severe Mercy* (New York: HarperOne, 2009), letter from Lewis to Vanhauken, (23, December, 1950), 93.

4. I refer to the thought experiment known as Schrödinger's cat, created by Austrian physicist Erwin Schrödinger which actually questions whether a poisoned cat in the box is dead or alive. Regardless, the point is the same without such finality to the cat.

5. I was influenced on this subject in part by Gary Zukav's, *The Dancing Wu Li Masters: An Overview of the New Physics*, (Fontana, 1980).

6. I didn't discover until years later that the views of 19th century Danish theologian Søren Kierkegaard—a rare Christian existentialist—held great promise.

7. Elson-Gray, *Dick and Jane Primer;* The Surprise Party (Scott Forseman, 1930's).

8. Ravi Zacharias is Founder and President of RZIM; rzim.org.

9. I was particularly impacted by a more streamlined version of this work: *Christianity for Modern Pagans: PASCAL's Pensées Edited, Outlined, and Explained,* by Peter Kreeft (Ignatius Press, 1993).

10. Ken Boa is the President of Reflections Ministries; kenboa.org.
11. See Bob Thomas', *Walt Disney: An American Original* (Glendale: Disney Editions, 1994).
12. For more information on Dr. William Lane Craig, see reasonablefaith.org.
13. For an accessible scientific refutation of the macro-evolution myth, I refer you to the delightful book, *Of Pandas and People: The Central Question of Biological Origins*, by Percival Davis and Dean H. Kenyon (Haughton Pub. Co., 1993).
14. During the publication of this book, my long-standing frustration over the Atlanta Falcons playoff drought was mercifully put to rest.
15. There is some debate as to whether this is an original quote from an interview, or perhaps an amalgamation of several quotes.
16. Usually attributed to Chinese philosopher Laozi (c 604 bc - c 531 bc).
17. Dallas Willard, *Hearing God* (Downers Grove, IL: InterVarsity Press, 2012), 185.
18. For those unfamiliar, this is a play on words from a speech given by actor Marlon Brando in the 1954 film classic, *On the Waterfront.*
19. C.S. Lewis, *God in the Dock* (Grand Rapids: Eerdmans Publishing Co., 1970), 13.
20. "Awake, O sleeper, and arise from the dead, and Christ will shine on you" (Eph 5:14b; ESV).
21. The list of such insightful writers and books is extensive. Notable among these are: *The Seeking Heart,* Francois

Fénelon; *Growing in Grace,* Bob George; *Lifetime Guarantee,* Bill Gillham; *The Spiritual Guide,* Michael Molinos; and *Handbook to Happiness,* Charles R. Solomon.

22. Major Ian Thomas, *The Indwelling Life of Christ: All of Him in All of Me* (Multnomah, 2006), 26.

23. Contrary to the chapter headings to Romans 7 inserted in various versions of the Bible, the verses say nothing about "two natures" fighting each other. As we're often reminded, the chapter titles of the Bible are later additions made for ease of study and are not on a par with Holy Scripture.

24. Francois Fénelon, *The Seeking Heart* (Jacksonville: SeedSowers, 1992).

25. *A Beautiful Mind,* directed by Ron Howard (Beverly Hills:Imagine Entertainment, 2001).

26. Adrian Rogers, Love Worth Finding Ministries; Radio sermon rebroadcast, 2013.

27. Brother Lawrence & Frank Laubach, *Practicing His Presence* (Jacksonville: SeedSowers, 1985)

28. Karate image courtesy of Gordon Dalbey, *Healing the Masculine Soul: God's Restoration of Men to Real Manhood* (Nashville: Thomas Nelson, 2003).

29. "Then God said, "Let us make man in our image, after our likeness. And let them have dominion over the fish of the sea and over the birds of the heavens and over the livestock and over all the earth and over every creeping thing that creeps on the earth" (Gen 1:26).

30. William Shakespeare, *Hamlet,* Act 3.

31. Significantly, a few days later Hal related that he had also sensed what seemed like a white light surrounding us on that day. This with no prior knowledge of my having experienced the same sensation.

32. Francois Fénelon, *The Seeking Heart* (Jacksonville: SeedSowers, 1992).

33. "Delight yourself in the LORD; And he will give you the desires of your heart" (Ps 37:4).

34. Henri J. M. Nouwen, *The Way of The Heart* (New York: Ballantine Books; Reprint Edition, 2003).

35. St. Teresa of Avila, *Interior Castle* (Mineola, New York: Dover Publications, 2007).

36. Mark J. Perry, *"AEIdeas,"* www.aei.org; American Enterprise Institute, February 26, 2014.

37. Adrian Rogers, Love Worth Finding Ministries; Radio sermon rebroadcast, 2012.

38. John Newton, "Amazing Grace," 1779.

39. Accuracy in reporting demands that I admit my daughter deserved to win on the occasion when she saw a bear worth fifty points. In retrospect, my tally of one-point squirrels seems an ignoble way to win.

40. Charles Solomon, *The Rejection Syndrome* (Carol Stream IL: Tyndale House, 1983).

41. Thomas Merton, *No Man is an Island* (Boston: Shambhala, 2005), 86.

42. The Five Stairsteps, "O-o-h Child," Buddha, 1970.

43. Danny O'keefe, "Good Time Charlie's Got the Blues," *O'keefe*, Signpost, 1972.

44. Larry Crabb, *Shattered Dreams* (Colorado Springs: WaterBrook Press, 2001), 57.

45. Henri J. M. Nouwen, *Life of the Beloved* (New York: Crossroad Publishing, 2002).

46. Adrian Rogers, Love Worth Finding Ministries; Radio sermon rebroadcast, 2012.

47. "A person's days are determined; you have decreed the number of his months and have set limits he cannot exceed" (Job 14:5; NIV).

48. C.S. Lewis, *The Problem of Pain* (New York: HarperCollins, 2001), 130.

49. Henry David Thoreau, *Walden* (Mineola, New York: Dover Publications, 1995).

50. Major Ian Thomas, *The Indwelling Life of Christ: All of Him in All of Me* (Multnomah, 2006), 57.

51. Eugene H. Peterson, *Run with the Horses* (Downers Grove, IL: InterVarsity Press, 2009), 39.

52. "The Allegory of the Cave" was first presented by the Greek philosopher Plato.

About the Author

Kevin Murray is the founder of Encourage to Faith Ministries. After twenty-eight years immersed in the commercial real estate world in Atlanta, Georgia, he left the familiarity of the company he co-founded to wholeheartedly follow his passion—encouraging others in their walk with the Lord. He is passionately engaged in sharing Christ-centered life principles through writing, teaching, speaking, and mentoring, all for the purpose of inspiring others to grow in their relationship with Jesus.

Originally from South Florida, Kevin moved to Atlanta, Georgia, where he received his BBA from Georgia State University. He and his wife, Karen, have four children and two grandchildren. In his free time, Kevin is an avid sports fan, marvels at nature, and most of all, enjoys building relationships.

Find Kevin at www.encouragetofaith.org.

Made in the USA
Lexington, KY
06 February 2017